MIDDLE SEA AUTUMN

BY MALCOLM MCCONNELL

W·W·NORTON & COMPANY   NEW YORK·LONDON

MIDDLE SEA AUTUMN

CAROL AND
MALCOLM McCONNELL

Published simultaneously in Canada by Penguin Books Canada Ltd, 2801 John
Street, Markham, Ontario L3R 1B4.
Printed in the United States of America.

The text of this book is composed in Janson Alternate, with display type set in
Ampurias. Composition and manufacturing by The Haddon Craftsmen, Inc.

Library of Congress Cataloging in Publication Data
McConnell, Carol.
  Middle sea autumn.
   1. Mediterranean Region—Description and travel.
  2. Boats and boating—Mediterranean Sea. 3. McConnell,
  Carol. 4. McConnell, Malcolm. I. McConnell, Malcolm.
  II. Title.
  D973.M38 1985 910'.091822 84–25526

ISBN 0-393-03304-X

W. W. Norton & Company, Inc., 500 Fifth Avenue, New York, N. Y. 10110
W. W. Norton & Company Ltd., 37 Great Russell Street, London WC1B 3NU

For
Doug Kane, a fine sailor
and a good friend

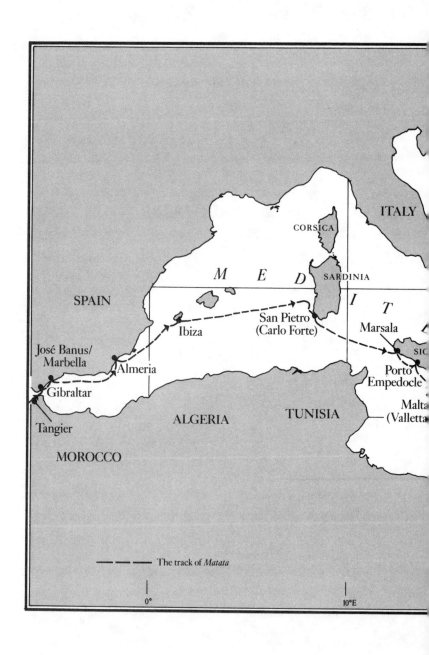

ITALY

CORSICA

SPAIN

M E D

SARDINIA

I T

José Banus/
Marbella

Ibiza

San Pietro
(Carlo Forte)

Marsala

SIC

Almeria

Porto
Empedocle

Gibraltar

ALGERIA

TUNISIA

Malta
(Valletta

Tangier

MOROCCO

———— The track of *Matata*

0°   10°E

CONTENTS

MIDDLE SEA AUTUMN

CHAPTER ONE

TANGIER, MOROCCO
SEPTEMBER 11, 1979

C arol and I were hot and winded after our long climb from
Tangier harbor to Boulevard Pasteur, the main business street
in the European quarter. Gratefully, we sank onto a cracked
cement bench on the promenade terrace that overlooks the harbor
and the blue channel of the Strait of Gibraltar.

As we sat in the sunshine, letting the sweat dry in the easterly
breeze, I studied the city around us. Tangier is built on the slopes of
a chalky limestone bluff above the strait. The town spreads in whitewashed terraces down the hillside to the modern apartment blocks
and hotels facing the palm trees and clapboard brochette stands on
the beach. To our left, fifteenth-century ramparts of beige sandstone
enclosed the Medina, the Muslim quarter surrounding the stout
brown fort of the Kasbah. The Medina is a cubistic jumble of flat-
roofed Moorish houses crowded above twisting medieval lanes. But

the new city where we rested consists mainly of white highrise buildings fronted by sidewalk cafés, along the avenue of palms.

Tangier is situated on the northwestern extremity of Africa. Sixteen miles across the strait, the tan mountains of Andalucia spill down to the sea. That is where Europe begins; or where it ends, depending on your perspective. Behind the whitewashed geometry of the city rise the green foothills of the Rif. South of the Rif, I knew, came the sun-blasted Middle Atlas; then the High Atlas; then the vast ocher wastes of the summer Sahara; then the thousands of verdant miles of tropical Africa. Cape Town was four thousand miles behind our backs, one-sixth of the way around the planet.

I squinted down at the wide concrete mole that curves like a Berber scimitar out into the harbor. At the foot of the mole lay the walled compound of Tangier port, a nondescript cluster of warehouses painted the mildewed mustard yellow that disfigures customs houses all across the Mediterranean world. In the middle of this jumble is the fishing port—two greasy jetties and a couple of rundown sorting sheds. From my vantage point, I could just distinguish the gleaming alloy mast of *Matata,* the Dufour Arpege sloop that we had sailed 3,700 miles across the Atlantic from a similar dilapidated pier—at Danny's boatyard in Brooklyn—to the crumbling concrete jetty down there in the harbor.

When we had tied up to the jetty, I had climbed ashore to wedge some fenders in between the rail and the rough cement and to lay out a couple of spring lines. The tide was down, and I had a good view of the boat, displayed below me as if it were beneath a walk-around gallery at a boat show. The white fiber glass decks and topsides were clean, though dull with brine. Rust stains bled from the tape-covered turnbuckles at the base of the shrouds, and the teak rail and trim were bone white, bleached by two months on the open Atlantic. But the running tackle and rigging were all in order. The life-raft canister and the bright red can of emergency water lashed to the coachroof, as well as the prominent plywood blade of the steering vane, gave *Matata* the definite flare of an ocean-going boat, a true passage maker. She is only thirty feet, length overall, but she is a strong and spirited little vessel and had carried us safely across the North Atlantic here to the doorway of the Med.

On the charts, the Atlantic Ocean officially did not end, or the Mediterranean Sea begin, until Europa Point, the southern tip of Gibraltar's shale ridge, twenty-four miles further east. But as far as Carol and I were concerned, we had at last crossed the bloody Atlantic and deserved a rest before plunging into the Med.

I yawned, shook my head and grinned with embarrassment, then yawned again, deeply, uncontrollably.

Carol smiled. "Me too," she said. "I'm *exhausted.*"

I nodded and took her strong, suntanned fingers in my hand. "At least that damn levanter has finally blown itself out."

She returned my nod. "Well, maybe we wouldn't have come here if we hadn't gotten so pounded by the storm. So, I guess we should be . . . well . . . thankful. . . . "

I scowled theatrically, then smiled in agreement.

For the previous three days and nights, we had tacked back and forth at the entrance of the strait, battered by a force-seven levanter that blew directly out of the east. When we had left the snug shelter of the marina at Vilamoura, Portugal, 250 miles northwest of the strait, at dawn on Saturday morning, September 8, we had anticipated a fifty-hour sail down the Spanish coast, through the strait, to the marina in Gibraltar. But by noon on Saturday the wind had backed around to the east, the sky had glazed over with cirro-stratus, and the barometer was sinking.

At dark that first night, with all manner of shipping converging on the entrance of the strait or barreling hell-bent into the Atlantic from the confines of the Med, we found ourselves double-reefed with a storm jib in a nasty, crashing, ten-foot swell, barely able to hold 180 degrees true, close-hauled. In retrospect, we now agreed, we should have turned around and headed back to the shelter of Vilamoura. But we had already cleared Portuguese customs and settled the marina bill. Returning would have meant a paperwork hassle and changing some of our dwindling reserve of precious green ten-dollar bills for relatively worthless escudos.

So, instead of exercising prudence, we had given in to naïve optimism. This blow, we reassured ourselves, could not be a true levanter

—one of those nasty five-day-or-more storms we had first encountered ten years before while living in Tangier. I had been a Foreign Service officer in charge of the American Cultural Center then, and Carol ran the U.S. Information Service English-teaching program. At the time we did not know much about boats or the sea. Windy autumn afternoons we would often stand on the terrace of our suburban villa, staring down the valley of Jews' River at the fishing trawlers and freighters fighting the chop and tide rips of the strait. Even though we had not then been experienced sailors, we had recognized the danger of a hard blow when it set against the main axis of the strait's tidal stream.

The eucalyptus trees would slash and creak in the wind, the sky would go gritty pink with Saharan sand, and the strait would become a crazy quilt of dirty whitecaps. We would sip our PX Scotch and smile anxiously down at the roller-coaster antics of the small coastal freighters and the fishing smacks, vaguely worried that the crews of those vessels might be in some kind of danger. Even then, however, we were aware of the nautical chronicles of such famous mariners as Horatio Nelson, stories replete with accounts of the square-rigged British fleet beating back and forth for *weeks* at the entrance to the strait.

Ten years later, we learned that a levanter in the strait was indeed dangerous to ships under sail and small vessels, and that this danger is readily explicable. Although our thirty-foot sloop was handier than a lumbering ship of the line, we were buffeted by the same laws of physics. The Mediterranean is a nearly landlocked sea; it is also bounded by desert coasts on its eastern and southeastern littorals. The Med loses much more water annually through evaporation than is replenished by rain or rivers. Thus a constant, massive influx of Atlantic water flows into the Med through the narrow and relatively shallow tube of the strait. Because of a difference in salinity, the Atlantic inflow current rides atop the denser, more saline outflow current that wells up and overflows the "sill" of the strait's bottom separating the Alboran Basin from the Atlantic proper. Tides, constricted by the steep, mountainous shores of Spain and Morocco, further complicate the hydrodynamics of the strait.

The net result of this situation for small-boat sailors caught in a full-scale levanter is nasty. When a 35- or 40-knot easterly wind is channeled by the Spanish and Moroccan mountains dead against the prevailing Atlantic inflow current, the sea becomes dangerously confused; when this pattern is further muddled by shifting tides, conditions can become such that a small sailboat like *Matata* simply cannot make safe headway into the strait. It becomes even more hazardous for such a small boat to tack north and south once inside the narrow confines of the strait because there are tide rips and "overspills" near both coasts. These latter hazards are associated with the complex currents generated by a strong levanter blowing during the monthly spring and neap tides, the conditions we had just sailed through.

Unfortunately for small boats, large modern ships are much less affected by these phenomena. The container ships, bulk carriers, and supertankers streaming nonstop through the strait are neither obliged by the rules of the road, nor really able, to take evasive maneuvers to avoid collision with thirty-foot sailboats. During a good levanter, with the face of the sea a field of curling white-crested swells, the white hull of a fiber glass sloop like *Matata* is virtually invisible from the bridge of a big tanker churning along at 25 knots.

If we had never learned the true nature of a levanter from the terrace of our comfortable, government-leased villa in 1969, we had sufficient remedial instruction during the seventy-two hectic, battering hours we spent beating between Cape Spartel and Cape Trafalgar, dodging fishing trawlers, container ships, reefers, and all manner of tankers, day and sleepless night. Finally, on the morning of the third day, we had felt the wind dropping and, with it, the sea. We shook out one reef, cranked up our small Volvo diesel and motorsailed around Cape Spartel, nine miles down the green and hilly Moroccan coast, and gratefully entered the calm water of Tangier harbor.

I stretched and stifled another yawn. It had been three days without any decent sleep, but we had ridden out the blow and we were safe. Visiting Tangier, as Carol had suggested, was in fact an unexpected bonus. When we had laid out our course from Vilamoura, we had chosen not to stop in Morocco even though we both loved

Tangier and had deep, pleasant memories of the two years we had lived there.

Because of various unforeseen problems inherent in any long passage in a small boat, we were badly behind our original schedule. It was now almost the middle of September, and we still had over 2,500 miles of sailing ahead of us before reaching our final destination: Lindos, on the Greek Aegean island of Rhodes. Furthermore, that long slog across the Mediterranean would be into the teeth of the prevailing autumn easterly storms, the levanters and siroccos of the post-equinox that traditionally have taken their toll on small vessels, from classical times right up to the present.

In short, we were in a hurry.

But today, we *were* in Tangier, so we decided we might just as well enjoy this unexpected sentimental excursion and look up old friends. I rose stiffly, lightheaded from the combination of little sleep and three days on a pitching, rolling, thirty-foot sloop. After six weeks at sea coming across the Atlantic, Carol and I were more sure-footed aboard the boat than we were ashore. Of course, the bottle of good Moroccan Boulouane Cabernet we had had with our steak and *pommes frites* at the modest Tangier Yacht Club probably added to my general giddiness. Whatever the cause, I was feeling decidedly odd, in a pleasant enough sort of way.

As I swayed above Carol's shoulder, gazing down at the pretty, white-washed town and the blue strait, I had a sudden flash of weird insight. It was as if I could *feel* the shape, the layout of the tectonic plates on which the continents and oceans alike were suspended, floating on the hot fluid magma of the earth's mantle. Tangier is one of those well-positioned sites on the earth where such a sudden geographic perception is not all that unusual.

Standing here on the extreme northern peninsula of Africa, staring across at the southern cape of Europe, was like being at similar global junctions, like Suez or Panama, maybe up in the Aleutians. I could almost physically sense the continental plates—the fragments of that primeval land mass the geologists call *Goanaland*—grinding together twenty or thirty miles under the soles of my scuffed sandals.

I could also sense the shape and extent of the visible land and water around us. Behind my back was Africa. Up there, beyond those tan Spanish mountains, Europe climbed away, over the curve of the earth, all the way to the Arctic ice cap, all that way east, to the vast flatlands of the Soviet Union. To the left, beyond the open blue bay spreading toward Trafalgar, lay the gray Atlantic. That was a body of water with which I felt a close, intimate connection on this last day of our forty-three days at sea. To the right, half hidden in evaporation haze, lay the soft aquamarine of the Mediterranean.

As I stared at the softer pastels of the Med, I felt myself literally turning my back on the gray void of the Atlantic. We were finished with that ocean. Two months earlier, we had still been gripped by the power of every cruising sailor's dream: a deep-ocean crossing in his own small ship. Now we had done it; we had sailed the Atlantic, arriving safely on the other shore with, as they say, all our faculties intact. This warm afternoon, I felt myself powerfully drawn further eastward, away from the rolling gray longitudes of the Atlantic and into the confines of the Mediterranean.

My lightheaded flashes of perception were passing, but not before I experienced a splintery insight into the elusive quintessence of the Mediterranean and of my own excitement at the prospect of sailing our boat across the length of that sea. I realized that my unlikely affinity for the Med came from a perfectly explicable desire to explore my own cultural roots. Not that I had any Mediterranean ethnic stock that I knew about. My personal connection to the Mediterranean world was less obvious, but just as valid a one as bloodlines. I was a citizen of a Mediterranean civilization: the United States of America.

Improbable as such insights might be at more rational moments, standing on that breezy terrace off Boulevard Pasteur in Tangier, staring down at the now-scattered whitecaps on the Strait of Gibraltar, I was held firm by the notion that America, a civilization shaped and guided by Greco-Roman philosophy and law and Judeo-Christian moral principles, was as much a Mediterranean colony in the twentieth century *anno Domini* as, say, Syracuse and Carthage had been colonies of successful Mediterranean states in the third century before Jesus of Nazareth; or, for that matter, Tangier, the Roman

Tingis, had been under the Emperor Augustus.

From a linguistic point of view, my language—English—was at least half Latin. My education had been acquired in institutions patterned on Greek and Roman models. My sense of civic duty and the responsibilities of citizenship, as well as the concept of the constitutionally constrained state, were clearly of Mediterranean origin. Having been raised a Roman Catholic in the days when the Mass was a Latin ritual, I could count that important aspect of my identity as being inarguably Mediterranean. Then, of course, the entire Euclidian, Pythagorian philosophical tradition of experimental science was the clear precursor of contemporary American technology. From a human perspective, this region, the Mediterranean Basin, was where I *came* from; I was not engaged in some arcane and hedonistic quest—sailing a small boat into the stormy autumn sea—I was simply, logically, coming home to my roots.

I smiled, then broke into an incongruous chuckle at my disjointed speculations. Obviously, I was a little punchy, more likely a little drunk, on half a bottle of strong Moroccan wine and a total of eight hours' sleep out of the previous eighty. Either we should move along and drink some more wine, I thought, or flag down one of those rickety little yellow Renault taxis and go back to the boat to get some sleep.

But, as I stood there in the sunny breeze, scenting the slightly mildewed, dead-flower spiciness of North Africa, I felt languidly immobile, unable to make a decision. I was glad that the levanter had blown when it did, glad that we'd been delayed here in Tangier. This was an ideal place to say goodbye to the Atlantic and to pause, contemplating the nature of the sea we were about to enter. The Mediterranean, I thought, "the sea between the lands"; that was the literal translation of the original Latin. In classical Greek it was **To Μασαιον**, the Middle Sea.

I pulled Carol up, using both hands to grip hers. Like me, she yawned. But her wide, blue-gray eyes were clear, almost as if she were well rested. Undoubtedly she was absorbed in her own thoughts and memories, maybe even in fanciful flights as odd as mine. Certainly we were both feeling the finality, the closure, of having sailed the North Atlantic Ocean, just the two of us, on a six-ton, thirty-foot machine made of plastic resins, glass fibers, steel, and wood. We were both also affected by the irony of being back in Tangier at the completion of an adventure the nature of which neither of us could have possibly imagined ten years earlier. When we had lived in Tangier in the late 1960s, we'd been considerably more conventional, and much less prone to adventure and risk taking. But then, in the spring of 1969, we had honestly and exhaustively discussed our true feelings about the direction in which our lives were going—seemingly without our controlling them—and decided that neither of us was temperamentally suited for government careers, even for relatively stimulating and exciting careers in the Foreign Service.

So, in one scary and invigorating rush of decisions, we resigned our positions, cashed in our retirement accounts, sold our trendy white Mustang fastback to an ambitious young Moroccan lawyer, withdrew our savings from the bank, and flew off to Greece, to the island of Rhodes and the whitewashed medieval village of Lindos, where we set to work to write the first of many Great American Novels. At the time—the optimistic crest of the hedonistic, egocentric 1960s—such a move seemed appropriate, maybe even a political statement about our own moral and intellectual independence from materialistic, dull government service. We were also both pushing thirty and wanted more from life than a secure pension and a progression of bronze ten-, twenty-, and thirty-year service pins.

Now we were both nearing forty; I had my birthday coming up in six days. We had, in fact, written several novels in those previous ten years; none, unfortunately, had been considered "great" by the critics. During our first five years in Greece, we had also learned to sail, first while crewing on a large charter yawl, then while running a sloop as a charter boat in partnership with a French friend. But that halcyon period of quiet prosperity in Lindos had eventually been quashed by the joint onslaught of inflation and mass tourism; our meager profits from writing and running the boat no longer paid the rent, and the village itself had degenerated into a garish, glittery travesty of its former self, at least for the five-month annual duration of the high tourist season. Where there used to be a quiet village *kafenion* in which we would sit with other writers late into the night sipping ouzo and feeding on free plates of *mezedes*, pontificating on Plato, Oscar Wilde, and the comparative virtues of Mao and Timothy Leary, there was now an abomination called "Yianni's Playland" that featured quad speakers blasting out the incongruous musical nonsense of the New Wave, while inside sullen English teen-agers hunched over tweaking and bonging video games.

We didn't really like Lindos in the summer anymore. But, we knew, the village did revert to its former uncrowded, quiet, and charming self each autumn and winter. It was our destination now. The previous winter we had been fortunate enough to experience an event of true rarity in the lives of contemporary writers: we actually made some money. In February, we had had an unusual confluence of royalty payments and an advance on a new book. Without too much soul searching, we had invested this bounty in a used Dufour Arpege sloop, outfitted the boat for an ocean crossing, and, in early July, set sail.

Our original plan had been to cross the Atlantic and be through the Med, safely ensconced in Lindos by October first, before the worst of the autumn storms struck. But, like most cruising plans, ours had encountered unforeseen delays. It was already the second week in September and, technically, we had not yet officially left the Atlantic. When I had taken a cursory look at the large British Admiralty Mediterranean Sea chart at the Vilamoura marina, I'd estimated the passage from Gibraltar to Lindos would take twenty-five full sailing days. With brief provisioning stops in the Balearic Islands, Sardinia, Sicily, Malta, and Crete, the sail across the Med to Rhodes would no doubt require a full six weeks, counting a *few* days holed up waiting out bad weather. It was now September eleventh. Our friend Doug Kane was due to join us in Gibraltar on the fourteenth for the sail across the Med. Realistically, I had to admit as Carol and I resumed our uneven progress along Boulevard Pasteur, we weren't going to make it to Lindos much before the end of October, a full month behind schedule.

I wasn't able to maintain the pessimistic tone of these musings very long, once we were caught up in the human current flowing down the wide sidewalks toward rue de la Liberté and the Medina. Tangier is a truly cosmopolitan city with an exotically mixed population that the old travelogue scriptwriters usually called a "colorful blend" of East and West. In fact, the city's position at the entrance to the Mediterranean and at the frontier between Christian Europe and the Muslim Maghreb has, over the previous centuries, guaranteed Tangier a polyglot, polyethnic population. The indigenous Riffi Berbers have been augmented by and commingled with Phoenicians, Carthaginians, Romans, Vandals, Visigoths, and Byzantines, then the Arabs of the Muslim invasion, and later Christian Spanish and Portuguese and British occupying powers. Because of its strategic position, Tangier was an International Zone for thirty years in this century, administered by a consortium of European nations and the United States. The town became part of the Kingdom of Morocco in the mid-1950s but has retained much of its traditional cultural mix.

Now, as we squeezed through the midday crowds on the sidewalk, I was reminded once again of the city's ethnic richness. A few meters ahead of us, a middle-class Moroccan Arab woman strolled along serenely, dressed in a long, tailored gabardine *djellaba* that culminated in a peaked hood, completely covering her head. Her face, of course, was hidden by a dark, gauzy veil. Beside this stylish matron walked her teen-age daughter. The girl wore designer jeans so tight they appeared to have been sprayed onto her well-proportioned legs. Her short-sleeved summer blouse was scooped revealingly both front and back, and her high-heeled sandals gave her a swaying, decidedly provocative gait.

Behind this mother and daughter, an old Berber lady hunched along, supporting a huge bundle of firewood on her bent back. The old woman wore the traditional leather leggings, straw sombrero-like hat, and candy-striped shawl first described by English travelers a hundred years before Columbus. All around us, street urchins with battered shoe-shine boxes or wire clips of dusty postcards scurried through the crowd, searching out tourists. In the roadway, donkey and horse carts, piled high with tomatoes or bright yellow melons, clumped along beside new Toyota pickup trucks and the station wagons of vacationing French families. There was a white Mercedes convertible making an illegal left turn and blocking oncoming traffic, the suave young Arab driver staring nonchalantly ahead through mirror sunglasses, oblivious to the cacophony of horns and the cries of the carters. Beside him in the front seat of the convertible sat a striking, suntanned girl who looked like a Scandinavian contestant in the Miss Universe contest. I turned to glance down the boulevard toward the post office and got a time-warp view of three bedraggled, long-haired backpackers with tattered jeans and tie-dyed T-shirts—stragglers perhaps from the Peace-and-Love days of the late sixties, washed up here in Tangier like frightened animals seeking an island shelter in a flooded forest.

No doubt about it, we were back in Tangier.

A small hand tugged at the side of my shirt. *"M'sieu, M'sieu,"* the little boy implored. *"Esoui chaussettes."* He flourished his gaudy orange shoe-shine box.

I smiled and pointed to my dusty, rather threadbare sandals. *"La, Mohammed, barakaloufique. M'shi debah. . . . Redah, insh'Allah."*

Inordinately proud of being able to resurrect some rusty phrases of Maghrebi Arabic, I beamed down at the shoe-shine boy as if I expected him to compliment me.

The kid scrutinized me for a few seconds while he scratched beneath the collar of his ragged Pepsi-Cola T-shirt. He was trying to identify my accent in Arabic. Without further hesitation, he answered in perfectly accented, post-hippie American English. "Okay, man . . . I'll catch you tomorrow."

He was gone into the crowd, his small head revolving like a radar dish, seeking out possible customers.

Carol laughed and squeezed my hand. "The shoe-shine boys haven't changed much," she said.

"They've gotten smarter maybe," I said, "if that's possible."

The last year we lived in Tangier, the Russian commercial fishing fleet began using the harbor as a liberty port on their way in and out of the Mediterranean from the Black Sea. Normally, the shoe-shine boys, pimps, souvenir vendors and assorted street Arabs, young and old, who plied their trades among the merchant seamen at the port, took it as a matter of normal *tanjaoui* chauvanism to address the sailors in their own language, whether it was English, Italian, Dutch, or Norwegian. However, during the first liberty of the Soviet fishing fleet outbound for the shoals off the Senegal River estuary, the young hustlers of Tangier port were stymied by the incomprehensible Russian. Yet, four weeks later, when the big sardine factory ship stopped on its way back to Odessa, the postcard hawkers and shoe-shine boys were wheeling and dealing in reasonably fluent Russian.

None of us diplomats or expatriates ever learned how those kids managed such a feat. Obviously there was more to it than just the cruel necessities of poverty and cut-throat competition. I like to think that somehow, over the centuries of almost incessant conquest by invaders of every outlandish stripe, the human gene pool in Tangier had evolved the useful survival adaptation of near-miraculous foreign language facility. Whatever the origin of this remarkable gift, the polyglot skills of the native Tangerois, as well as the complex cultural mosaic of the town, made Tangier an exciting place to live.

I realized, as we swung onto the terrace of the Café de Paris to take a little liquid sustenance, that Tangier was quintessential Med, a microcosm of the larger Mediterranean world. Here the Latin and the Arab, the Levantine and the Berber, commingled, cross-pollinated. Here, one Mediterranean civilization after another had swept across this limestone ridge and paused for a brief period to watch the gray Atlantic slide into the blue Mediterranean. In Tangier, we would often stop for *pinchitos* (brochettes) at the Socco Chico (Suq el Sehrir) before attending a concert at the Centre Culturel, then dine out on a meal of *couscous* and *tagine* accompanied by excellent Moroccan rosé, and end up the evening shooting darts and quaffing pinks or bitters in an English pub. In the course of such a normal evening, we would have spoken French, Spanish, a smattering of Arabic, and, of course, English.

During our second summer living in Tangier in the late sixties, one of Carol's cousins came to visit us. Sandy had just graduated from secretarial school in Milwaukee and had never traveled much outside the Midwest. Her parents put her on a plane and fifteen hours later she arrived, just in time to join us at Countess Louise de Marron's annual August party for five or six hundred of her dearest friends among the Tangier expatriate community and the migrating flocks of European jet-setters who descended on the town each summer.

Toward midnight, when a hundred or so half-naked revelers representing probably ten nationalities and races were careening around a bonfire, sucking on champagne bottles or *kif* pipes, led by a band of professional J'Naoua dancers from the Sahara, Sandy stood literally as wide-eyed and virtually as slack-jawed as Dorothy in the Land of Oz.

"Do you . . . ah, do you have these kind of *parties* very often?" she asked.

Joe Kimmins, a Peace Corps friend stationed in Tangier, and one of the resident wits among the young expats, was gallant enough to answer her: "Only on weekends."

But that torchlit night, with the jasmine heavy in the moonlight and the bronze clankers and *tabla* drums of the J'Naoua blocking out all rational thought, was over ten years ago. The crazy, prosperous sixties were behind us. We no longer lived in glittery Tangier or sunny Lindos. For the past three years I had been working on a long, commercially worthless novel and paying the rent by teaching creative writing as writer-in-residence at various universities. Teaching creative writing at midwestern backwater colleges was not quite as exciting as joining a drunken, impromptu conga line behind Ursula Andress. Plowing through upstate New York blizzards to teach bored freshmen the rudiments of English composition at St. Lawrence University was nowhere near as much fun as writing fiction in the whitewashed medieval tower of our first house in Lindos.

But we were now in the era of shrinking resources and limited possibilities that all the gloom merchants had been predicting for the last two decades of this century. Carol and I had a chance to steal a few months back in Lindos before being forced back onto the academic treadmill. We had a chance to live a simple, healthy life in the sun, near the sea, in a house that did not have to be triple-locked each night to keep out the burglars and rapists. All we had to do to reach this temporary haven from the predictable pressures and problems of the twentieth century was sail our boat twenty-five hundred miles across the Mediterranean Sea . . . during the fall storm season, against the track of the easterly weather.

As I sipped my second glass of iced rosé in the Café de Paris, I realized that a lot of harassed taxpayers from New Jersey to Oregon would gladly have traded places with us right then. But I also realized that such a swap was impossible. If that little sloop down at the greasy pier in the fishing harbor was ever going to swing on an anchor in Lindos harbor, we were going to have to sail it there ourselves.

STRAIT OF GIBRALTAR
SEPTEMBER 12, 1979
1040

The bow rose up, then smacked down with such speed and so much violent noise that Carol peered up through the half-open companionway hatch. I ducked some stinging spray and hung on to the tiller with both hands. We heeled hard to port and fell off another steep swell.

"Shit," I muttered. When were we ever going to get a break with the weather. For two hours we had been tacking north toward the Spanish lighthouse at Tarifa and back south again toward the Moroccan light at Cape Malabata. For at least the past ninety minutes it had been clear to me that this morning's fluky easterly breeze had degenerated into a mini-levanter.

We had left Tangier harbor later than our scheduled 0700 departure time, a little hung over but well rested. In the muddle of customs formalities and chatting up the port police, I'd forgotten to check the port captain's office for a weather report. I had checked the tide table and noted that slack water would turn to the eastbound, inward tide at 0940. If we were lucky, I figured, we'd get about 3 free knots, and, even motor-sailing, we'd arrive in Gib in early afternoon.

But the breeze had built steadily for two hours, and now we had a reef in the main and it was pretty obvious the working jib was too much headsail, judging from the angle of heel and the violent smacking every time a strong gust hit us. I pulled the hood of my oilskin jacket closer around my face and hunkered down under the leecloth. The steering vane was sailing the boat well enough, so there was not much I had to do. A half-mile behind us, a steady line of shipping —tankers, container vessels, and freighters of various ilks—rumbled due west, Indian file in the northern separation lane, bound out of the Med and into the Atlantic. We had a mile or so to go to the brown and rocky Spanish coast. Tacking this way, trying to make ground against the wind, we had to cross both the inbound and outbound shipping lanes twice on each set of tacks. I swore again.

The rhumb-line course from Tangier harbor to Europa Point at Gibraltar was only twenty-four miles, four hours on a decent day. But here we were, about to get hit with the same conditions that had prevailed for three days straight during the bad levanter: 30 knots of easterly wind against the strong inflowing spring tide. That would become dangerous quickly. We might well run out of daylight tacking back and forth in the crazy swells, then find ourselves in trouble with all this shipping.

I cursed loudly, and Carol slid back the hatch. She climbed out, dropped down on the cockpit bench opposite me and snapped up her oilskins. "The tide's swinging against the wind," she said, scowling at the dirty crested swells.

Standing, I braced myself against the close-hauled boom and mainsheet. "It sure as hell is," I muttered. Then, reluctantly, I scanned the narrow horizons, taking some spray in my eyes as I did so. "I think we'd better head back to Tangier," I said, speaking slowly so as to not betray my disappointment. Here we were, having just completed a strenuous Atlantic crossing, about to turn back from a crummy little 30-knot blow. But there was no mistaking the logic of the decision. Seamanship is, no matter what old yacht club salts like to pretend, not a very complicated business. The decision was obvious.

Good seamanship involves preparation of the vessel and crew as well as prudence. That morning, bleary-eyed and groggy from a late night with friends at the Parade Bar, we had exercised neither. Now we were on the edge of a hazardous situation. Our course of action was clear: tack around and reach back to Tangier before conditions got much worse.

Had this been the Atlantic, we could simply have borne off twenty more degrees and sailed long, five-hour tacks, full and by, comfortably clipping angles off the rhumb-line course. But we were no longer in the open ocean.

Carol slid along the bench to the headsail sheet winch. She held the salty, braided line in her fingers, looking over her shoulder for the signal. I nodded somberly. "Okay," I said, "stand by . . . ready about. . . ."

We were through the wind and sailing nicely on a course of 190 degrees true, an easy beam reach back toward the geometric white heap of Tangier, spread across the green foothills of the Rif. Ahead of us the long column of shipping churned on. I knew we had made the right decision, but it still rankled. Similar conditions of constricted channels with dangerous tidal patterns existed in several parts of the Med. If we let ourselves get turned around every time the wind headed us, we'd never make it to Greece before Christmas.

Carol must have sensed my exasperation. She reached across and took my hand. "We'll have a nice lunch when we get back in," she said, smiling. "Then we can sleep all afternoon and get a good early start."

I gazed around the boat. With this wind on the beam we were riding much more smoothly, almost as if the sea were mocking us. But such thoughts were the old paranoia, generated by fatigue and worry, that I'd known so well out in the Atlantic during those gales. Carol was right; some more sleep was in order.

STRAIT OF GIBRALTAR
SEPTEMBER 13, 1979
0800

We powered through the foggy morning on mainsail and engine, due east, right down the middle of the separation lane in the center of the strait. Dead ahead the sun hung like an orange spotlight, weakened by the fog to a warm disc. Visibility was about a thousand yards, and extending slowly as the force of the sun increased. We could not yet see the Spanish coast, however, and Tangier and the green slopes above Cape Malabata had disappeared astern. We were sailing on a compass heading of 98 degrees, 90 degrees true, directly through the center of the strait.

If our piloting had been anywhere near accurate, the westbound shipping lane was a mile north of us, and the inbound, eastward lane was a mile to the south. I turned, my cleated sea boots slipping on the fog-wet cockpit sole. There were ships out there to both port and starboard, ghosting through the fog, unseen. I could hear them clearly, their engines thumping like distant kettle drums. Up on the portside spreader, the gold-foil plates of the radar reflector twisted languidly in the fog. Fat condensation droplets splattered down off the mainsail. A foghorn on a ship hooted four times. I swallowed and sat down.

Carol was crouched on the port side of the cabintop, peering ahead with the binoculars. If there was any danger of collision, we reasoned, it would come from the westbound ships plunging toward us. But we hoped not. As long as we were where we thought we were —in the middle of the strait—we wouldn't be in any trouble from the large, fast ships that were plowing along at cruising speed on radar bearings. The tide was still slack and would swing east in about an hour. The barometer was high and steady, and, we knew, there was a cloudless sky up above this persistent fog bank that filled the strait.

Both our main bulkhead compass and the hand-bearing one were reliable instruments. If we didn't encounter any unusual currents, we wouldn't be pushed north or south. All I had to do was keep my eye on the white-etched black wheel of the compass card and steer the boat. Beneath my boots, the dependable Volvo Penta diesel thumped along at two-thirds revs: cruising speed of 5 knots. When the tide swung, we'd pick up a knot or two. The sea was flat this morning with no residual swell from yesterday's blow. We could not see land to take bearings, but our dead reckoning was usually accurate and we were trailing our Walker taffrail log, so that we would know when to turn north for Algeciras Bay and Gibraltar.

The seamanship problems this morning were minimal, yet there was a certain spookiness about the sunlit, milky weight of the fog bank and the unseen rumbling of the nearby ships. If I took my eyes from the compass and stared ahead into the bright dome of mist for more than a few seconds, I felt a kind of horizontal vertigo, a disorientation; the bow would swing north or south of the course as if pulled by the magnetic influence of the unseen steel in the ships' hulls. Spooky. I knew that part of my problem was a kind of claustrophobia. For over forty sailing days we had enjoyed the unencumbered expanse of the open sea. Now, we could feel the constricting presence of land around us; not simply land, but shoals, reefs, rocks, submerged wrecks—in short, all the nasty coastal obstacles we would have to cope with for the next 2,500 miles. Welcome to the Med.

"See anything?" I called to Carol.

She took another slow scan with the glasses, then shook her head. "Just fog. But you sure can hear them out there, can't you?"

"How about taking the tiller for a while?" I asked. "I'm getting dizzy."

Carol clumped down into the cockpit, her bright blue sea boots slipping as mine had on the greasy, salt-fog condensation. She had a vaguely troubled expression as she took the helm. Away to the south, we heard a churning, washing-machine kind of noise. We exchanged glances, and I took the binoculars from around her neck. She ducked slightly to help me lift the glasses free, and, as she did so, I realized how natural, how automatic, such actions had become between us. We now worked together almost as a single unit; rarely did we have to exchange formal commands or instructions when we went through the workaday functions of sailing.

Now we stood shoulder to shoulder, our damp oilskin jackets touching as we peered to starboard, toward the source of the strange noise.

"Hydrofoil."

"Hydrofoil."

We both spoke the word at the same instant as the outlandish, tubular white hull of the Tangier-Gibraltar hydrofoil appeared out of the solid fog bank and cut diagonally across our course, steering ten degrees north of our heading. The vessel reminded me of a crude model spaceship from a Buck Rogers serial at the Bay Theater in Milwaukee in the early forties. All that was missing were the sparkler trails of smoke and the poorly hidden supporting ropes. But this strange little ship was not a stage prop. It was made of real steel, and that bottle-nosed bow could instantly crush our sailboat in a collision.

Carol instinctively fell off a few degrees to port, but the reflex was of no importance. The hydrofoil was making over 20 knots. It was gone out of sight almost as quickly as it had appeared, a bizarre apparition of a rusty white hull riding atop stilt-like foils, its engines sounding more like an old-fashioned wheat thresher than a ship. Before the hydrofoil disappeared completely, however, I saw that he had two radar dish antennas scanning rapidly on his short radio mast above the airliner bridge. Just as it reentered the fog bank, the hydrofoil cut loose with a siren blast. Carol and I both flinched.

"Weird," she said. "I wonder if he had us on radar."

I shrugged, then glanced at the slowly spinning gold disc of the radar reflector. "People say those things aren't really much good. I think I'll run the strobe light up the shroud. That'll make us a little more visible."

Carol seemed unconvinced, subdued by the sudden appearance of the hydrofoil and its equally precipitous disappearance. She might well have been pondering the reality that our chosen hobby, our serious avocation of offshore cruising and passage making, was, in fact, replete with life-threatening risks. Or maybe I was just projecting my own anxiety.

As I tied the red plastic shaft of the man-overboard strobe onto the flag halyard at the portside shrouds, I kept up a barrage of cheerful smalltalk, trying to lighten the moment, to dilute the fog bank that encircled us with its strangely intermixed sunlight and gloom. But it was Carol who managed to change our mood. Pointing aft, she smiled broadly and sang out, "Dolphins . . . look, Malcolm, a whole big herd."

Indeed it was. They were small, gray Atlantic dolphins, calves with their cows, a few larger, darker gray bulls—lots of them, certainly more than fifty. They splashed toward us in the milky sunlight, porpoising like all dolphins, the whole herd steadily moving from port to starboard across our bow, like improbable commuters on some unseen freeway, heading in for another day at work. The show was charming; we both love animals and have spent a lot of our married life together in African game parks and preserves and in zoos all over the world. We never really get tired of watching wild animals leading their normal, wild lives like these dolphins.

Carol reached down with the toe of her boot and slid the throttle arm up so that the boat slowed to a power idle. The dolphins splashed along, fifty yards off the port side, squeaking audibly now, gleaming wet in the watery sunglow.

"Look," Carol said, pointing again with outstretched arm.

A cow dolphin broke free of the surface with two small, pearl-gray calves at her side, keeping perfect pace as they plunged into the rippled surface and broke free again a moment later.

We stood there on the deck of our boat, completely taken by the display. Then the shiny, lithe creatures were gone into the top-lit fog bank off to starboard. I secured the flag halyard and swung back along the port side toward the cockpit. Carol stooped to advance the engine throttle. For no particular reason, I found myself staring back aft, off the port quarter, into the dimmer fog away from the sun.

I stopped, one foot inside the cockpit, one still on the coachroof, my fingers gripping the wet alloy boom. A ponderous black-and-white killer whale broke the surface a hundred yards away, porpoising slowly through the same water the dolphin herd had just traversed. The Orca was glossy black, with a heavy, rounded head and a towering blade of a dorsal fin. It silently reentered the sea, then rose again, wafting a snort of steam through its blow hole. As I stood, paralyzed with mixed fear and admiration, another Orca appeared behind the leader, then two more. Each wore the guileless, disarming harlequin colors of stuffed nursery pandas. As the thirty-foot bull glided heavily past our bow, his shiny black eyeball rotated slightly within the white oval surrounding his eye socket. For a moment, he kept us both in his atavistic gaze, then the eye shifted forward, no longer interested in a small sailboat or the two boney, upright creatures on its deck.

I licked my dry lips. Carol was in a crouch, transfixed by the sight of the four killer whales. They blew a ragged volley; they rose and fell; they moved at their steady, unhurried pace, trailing the herd of dolphins with their hypersensitive hearing and their echo-ranging sonar.

When they were gone into the fog bank, I descended the rest of the way into the cockpit and reached down unsteadily to advance the throttle. Carol rubbed her fingers nervously across her throat. I took the tiller.

"Get the flare gun," I said as evenly as my tight chest muscles would permit, "and the air horn."

Carol nodded without answering and slipped into the companionway. Our flare pistol fired 25MM exploding rockets. It was our only real weapon, but it was probably sufficient to ward off the killer whales should they change their minds and decide to stalk us instead of the dolphins. The air horn was not a weapon per se, but I knew that the loud blast, sounded underwater, was a devastating discouragement to all whales.

Carol climbed back to the cockpit quickly, clutching the air horn and the black plastic box of the flare pistol. She grabbed the tiller while I loaded the flare gun and snapped shut the heavy, reassuringly wide barrel of the weapon. These precautions, I suddenly realized, were more of psychological value than anything else. If the Orcas wanted to attack, they could come in a rush of submerged power that would literally overturn us in a second, capsizing the boat and throwing us into the water. My precautions with the flare gun and air horn were therefore worthless. But I did feel a certain satisfaction, hefting the comforting weight of the pistol in my two hands.

We leaned close, our shoulders touching again, both self-consciously aware of our own fright, and both embarrassed by it. Killer whales, we knew, were normally not interested in sailboats, especially during daylight when the pack could visually identify prey. But, there was something frightening, fundamentally evil in those huge predators' beguiling panda disguises. Their jaws, we knew, held parallel rows of teeth as long and sharp as any K-bar commando knife. If they decided we looked like prey, we would quickly become a meal.

We waited, armed with our silly little flare gun and our air horn. The engine rumbled and bubbled along, the fog became gradually lighter as the sun rose. Then, in an instant, we were out in the clear. The parallel ridges of Spain and Morocco lay sharply defined in the morning sunlight. The rows of shipping were right out there, too—big green tankers and yellow container ships, coasters with splotches of red lead on their hulls, even a couple of clean white refrigerator ships outbound with fresh produce from Algeria.

We stripped off our oilskins, and I went forward to take down the swaying strobe light from the flag halyard on the portside spreaders. I held the helm while Carol fetched a couple of icy beers. The tan smear of Gibraltar was right where it should be, fine on the port bow. What a beautiful, benevolent morning; what a Mediterranean morning. Finally. The gray Atlantic was behind us.

We sipped our beers and chatted about nothing in particular; then, Carol turned to look astern, toward the dull white slope of the fog bank we had just left.

"Oh my God. . . . " Her voice was throaty, truly afraid.

The black sail of the submarine was tall and lean, like the dorsal fin on the bull Orca. The sub was awash, cruising directly behind us at about 15 knots, its black sail the only visible metal above the water. On the bridge, three officers leaned their elbows in a row, like perching starlings, studying us with their glasses. The sub made no noise, cast no exhaust trail. It was a nuclear vessel, I saw, a hunter-killer, the technological equivalent of the bull Orca we had seen ten minutes before.

As we watched, virtually spellbound, the officers disappeared one by one. The sub seemed to slow, then it was lowered as if on a hydraulic lift. Then it was gone, completely, not even a war-movie giveaway trace like a periscope, just an oily width to the water where the sub had been.

"Did . . . " Carol's voice was coming back. "Did you *see* that thing?"

"I sure did. I think he was a Russian."

Carol peered ahead, as if to study the sea where the sub was now riding, submerged. "Do you really think so?"

I shrugged. "Those guys on the bridge looked, well . . . sinister."

"Do you realize," she said, sitting down now and cupping her beer bottle in both hands, the morning sunlight making her hair shine reddish-brown, "Do you . . . that sub is down there right now, with the dolphins and the killer whales. They're all . . . well, they're all sort of swimming together."

I had another bizarre insight: the biological sonar of the small and large toothed whales, interfacing, as they say, with the electronic pinging from the black domes at the bow of the nuclear sub. Human beings, whose technological roots were directly traceable back to this pastel blue sea basin that we were about to enter, had progressed in the twenty centuries since Western civilization began to define itself as a superior entity: we now harnessed the powers inherent in the very fabric of the universe to hunt each other beneath the dark waves, just as did our primitive relations, the supposedly mindless whales.

Ahead of us, the fortified mound of Gibraltar shone in the bright sun like a steel anvil.

CHAPTER TWO

GIBRALTAR
SEPTEMBER 13 TO 22

≈≈≈≈≈

I LOOKED AT MALCOLM grasping the tiller behind me. He was smiling. I too was relieved to have finished with the Atlantic. Officially we were now in the Mediterranean, and it felt like coming home. Europa Point stood off the starboard beam, and the city of Gibraltar was emerging from the haze ahead. Far off to port, the white smear of Algeciras rippled across the bay like a mirage, then faded out. We weren't in yet; we had to ease our way through the shipping in the roadstead, find the marina, and get ourselves docked. None of the charts we had on board gave any details of the harbor, so we'd have to feel our way in.

"Another sub," Mal said, pointing, "but one of 'ours.' "

I followed his stare, shuddering as the silent, murky image of the Russian sub superimposed itself on the slightly rolling gray metal tube tied up just inside the harbor wall. Beyond the sub, several destroyers were neatly moored alongside the wide quay. Slim spars poked skyward above the ships' stubby masts and radio towers. Obviously the marina was around the next sea wall, tucked in between the destroyer pens and the air strip. It was time to drop sail.

We backed into the slip the marina attendant indicated. Customs officials would come to us soon, he said, tying off our two lines. I hoped we wouldn't have too long to wait. Meanwhile, I began to straighten up down below . . . opening the hatches and rinsing the glasses . . . the usual housekeeping chores on board a boat when you arrive in port.

In Horta on the island of Faial in the Azores, and again in Vilamoura, we had met up with Chris Schultz on *Tao Loa* and his friends June-Marie, Jeffrey, and Karen. They, too, sailed a Dufour, a thirty-five footer. Now I heard Malcolm hoot a greeting and, popping my head up the companionway hatch, saw Jeffrey and Karen approaching us with what looked like a couple of cold beers. They couldn't come on board yet, not until we had been inspected by a customs agent and the health authorities, but we chatted to them on shore as we drank our beer.

"What happened to you?" Jeffrey asked. We had left three days before them from Vilamoura. They had missed the levanter completely and had powered through the strait directly to Gibraltar, arriving that morning.

Malcolm and I stared at each other. We could have avoided those three miserable days of beating into the levanter if we had waited. But then, we wouldn't have revisited Tangier.

By early evening, we had signed in at the marina office and paid our fees. I had luxuriated in the public showers next to the office, enjoying the unlimited quantity of hot water. While Malcolm checked at the harbor master's office for our mail, I shopped at the small supermarket just outside the port gate. When we met, Malcolm had bad news. The check we were so sure would be here, forwarded by his agent, had not yet arrived. Our small supply of green dollars was dangerously low after my shopping excursion.

June-Marie was sitting in our cockpit waiting for us when we returned to *Matata.* "We're going pub crawling. Chris and Jeffrey already checked it out and there must be twenty pubs right on Main Street. Wanna come?"

I saw that she was already dressed for shore in a neat sun dress, her sandals lined up on the dock. Mal and I would have to change, ten, fifteen minutes. . . . Glancing up at Mal as he helped pull in the stern lines so I could hop aboard, I saw the disappointment in his face. Of course we couldn't go out. "I'm sorry, June-Marie, but I think we're pretty tired tonight."

"Right," Mal said behind me. "Maybe another night."

"Sure. Okay." June-Marie got up to leave. "You're sure?"

When she had gone, we sat in the cockpit sipping our cheap Moroccan wine. I could smell food cooking on some of the boats around us, but I didn't feel like going below quite yet and starting our dinner. In fact, I didn't want to cook at all.

"You're not really tired?" Malcolm asked.

"No, it's just the money."

"I know." Mal poured more wine in our glasses. "Rotten luck. Gibraltar is a fun place."

We had trouble making conversation as we got more and more depressed.

"What the hell," Mal said, "let's go, we can catch up with them." He smiled his best, brightest smile at me.

I lifted my glass to him in a mock toast. "Here's to Gibraltar. Let's go."

Perched on the concrete parapet, the sun warm on our faces, Carol and I gazed down at the rooftops of Gibraltar town. Main Street curved along the base of the limestone bluff, a dense spread of nondescript commercial blocks and apartments broken occasionally by parks and palm-lined squares. The architecture was a rather unpleasant hodgepodge of Spanish stucco, British brown institutional, and ersatz Miami.

Above us, the asphalt road cut switchbacks into the sheer gray limestone of the Rock's eastern face. There was wind-twisted shrubbery further up, stunted cedars, and the thorny *maquis* of the dry Mediterranean littoral. Partially hidden by this scrub brush, the thick concrete shields of the gun sites and the radar antennae were hard to see. But we knew they were up there; Gib's raison d'être resided in those long-barreled cannons, and, of course, in the tan cement geometry of the destroyer pens and naval dockyards that dominated the waterfront. Off to the right, as far as we could see from our vantage point halfway up the cliff, was the southern edge of the airport's single runway, thrust out into the pale water of Algeciras Bay on a rubbly base of landfill.

Between the airport and the docks lay the crowded marina. *Matata* was tied up in an inner slip, but there were too many other small white sailboats for us to distinguish ours.

We had climbed the Rock to get some exercise after a heavy pub meal of shepherd's pie and pints of bitter. The excursion also had another, less obvious purpose. The telephone-telegraph office would not open until after the long summer siesta, so we had a couple of hours to fill, and neither of us felt like sitting on the boat. Nor were we inclined to stay in the Main Street pub; the barroom had filled with pink-faced British sailors who all looked about thirteen years old, despite the tangles of gaudy tattoos on their arms and the speed with which they chugged down brimming mugs of stout and bitter. The place soon fogged up with cigarette smoke, and the pounding, intentionally abrasive punk rock made sitting anywhere near the stereo jukebox impossible.

Personally, I wouldn't have minded easing my diffuse but swelling money anxiety with a few more beers and a long snooze under *Matata*'s sun awning. But that was pure escapism. The fact was that our protracted financial problems were, apparently, worse than we'd anticipated: the royalty check from my literary agent that we had been *certain* would be with our mail at the harbor master's office had not been among the bills and family correspondence.

Now it seemed that there'd be no magical check to replenish our cash supply. We did, of course, have a little credit remaining on our various American charge cards, but that wouldn't help with supermarkets in Gibraltar or Spain.

Our phone calls later that afternoon would answer several questions for us, not the least of which being if we could prevail on LaVerne, Carol's mother, for yet another "emergency" loan to bail us out until the Viking check reached us in Greece. LaVerne was, of course, extremely generous, but it irked me unreasonably to have to call home like a college kid stranded in Fort Lauderdale to borrow money. I was not a college kid. In three days, I would be forty years old.

Carol, as usual attuned to my shifting moods, reached over and stroked the back of my clenched fist.

"Don't worry," she said. "I'm sure a thousand will get us to Greece, and Mom's already said she was keeping that in reserve in case we needed it.￼

I did not immediately answer, nor did I feel inclined to squeeze her sun-warm hand. Below us, a modern fleet oiler painted the light gray of the Royal Navy lay alongside in the dockyard. It was from that ship that the teen-age British ratings had descended on the pub. By this time, they'd probably be blotto, staggering back on board to pass out in their bunks, their brief liberty considered a great success. For a moment, I actually envied the simple irresponsibility of their lives. They were protected, taken care of by a system. After working the week at their mindless tasks in the deck department or engine room, they pulled on their white sailor suits, came ashore, got drunk, then returned to the bland, secure matrix of the fo'c'sle, which, these days, offered color TV, hot showers, and air conditioning, not to mention a daily tot of rum and plenty of free food.

I pictured the faculty lounge of the English department at Purdue University . . . bland institutional paint on the walls, anonymous prints of Georgian villages, splayed Naugahyde furniture: a comfortable American fo'c'sle—a cloying, but protective, matrix. In January, I would be back there, teaching creative writing on my second stint as writer-in-residence. Next fall, I'd take up similar duties at the El Paso branch of the University of Texas.

This time we had now, crossing the Atlantic and sailing our boat on to Greece, was *our* liberty, our furlough away from banal imperatives of modern civilization, from insurance premiums and Master Card bills and IRS form 1040. Instead of regretting the necessity of borrowing money to see us on to Greece, I should be grateful that LaVerne was able and willing to help us. This trip was *stolen time*, six months snatched away from the grinding, inevitable juggernaut of middle-class responsibility.

I turned and took Carol's hand between both my palms. "Let's go back and have a nap," I said. "We can call tonight when it's afternoon in the States. We really are going to be okay, as long as we don't start panicking."

Carol nodded soberly, a concise gesture of agreement that wordlessly acknowledged the problems of the weeks ahead—weather and a minimum of cash. She looked at me with her calm blue eyes and nodded again. "Well," she said, breaking her contemplative silence, "we got across the Atlantic. We can't let the Med stop us, can we?"

The black boat, a "cigarette," as these long, low, incredibly fast craft are called, rumbled slowly along the channel and slid up to the marina fuel dock. Slouched behind the wheel in the low-slung cockpit, the young man scowled at the large NO SMOKING sign above the gas and diesel pumps, looked away with feigned boredom, and proceeded to puff on his cigarette. From my perspective on the dock, I could look across the bows of two sailboats and observe him without betraying my scrutiny. Earlier, Carol had pointed out the three lean black speedboats as the probable source of the cacophonous engine howl and sudden, slapping wake that had disturbed the people sleeping in the marina's boats at dawn that day.

When I had first seen the three boats, rafted together at the end of the jetty, I'd assumed that they were some kind of crash boats, attached to the RAF station at the nearby airport. But, coming out of the showers five minutes before, I had noticed that they bore no names, registration numbers, or national ensigns. I'd also recognized the nubby black texture of their decks and topsides: military radar-absorbing paint—expensive, and unavailable on the civilian market.

The last time I'd seen such a paint job had been on a CIA Swift boat during the Simba Rebellion in the Congo, in 1965.

But, watching the young helmsman as he secured his bow and stern lines to the fuel jetty, I was reasonably certain he was not part of any government intelligence service. He looked like a smuggler to me. A moment later, he was joined by three other men, and my suspicion became conviction. If a casting agent in Century City needed four contemporary smugglers, these guys were shoo-ins for the parts. All were brawny and deeply tanned from hours spent in open boats. They bore the usual collection of service tattoos, but their features were immeasurably harder than the teen-age sailors in the pub. Two were swarthy; two, sun-bleached fair. All four wore dark slacks and black T-shirts.

With languid grace, the largest of the four hopped into the boat and opened the clamshell covers of the two engine compartments, aft of the small cockpit. I could just distinguish the chromed barrels of the dual carburetors on one supercharged V-8 engine. No wonder the early-morning engine snarl had awakened us: each of those boats had almost a thousand horsepower in its engines, enough speed to evade even the fastest naval patrol vessel.

Now the shorter of the two fair-haired men was down in the cockpit, gesturing to his mate, who seemed to be adjusting some linkage on the throttles of the port engine. Their speech was incomprehensible glottal-stop cockney, but I could catch the regular ebb and flow of jocular obscenity that served as a link for the otherwise disjointed nouns and verbs.

Years before, while serving at the American Consulate General in Tangier, I'd read Interpol reports of organized groups of smugglers using high-speed boats to move large amounts of contraband between Spain and North Africa. At the time, I had dismissed much of the speculation as overly romantic; surely the authoritarian Franco government and the efficient Royal Navy in Gib would break up any *regular* widespread smuggling operation. Apparently, however, such operations were still viable and, judging by the eighty or ninety thousand dollars invested in these three boats, highly profitable.

When they finished their fueling and engine adjustments, each man took his station at the wheel of a boat, and the short blond stood behind the driver of the largest of the three. This boat had a small Decca radar antenna mounted on a stout black fiber glass mast. On a nod from their leader, the three drivers started their engines, and the boat basin echoed with the popping roar of the exhausts.

They slipped their lines and crawled away down the narrow channel, dead slow, dragging with them a harsh dome of engine noise. Just clear of the marina, the blond leader signaled again, and the boats dug in their heels and pounded into Algeciras Bay on dirty white rooster tails, their exhaust scream echoing off the face of the Rock far above. High on the limestone cliffs, the last of the sun was fading from amber to gray. In one hour, it would be full night out in the strait. The moon would not rise until after midnight. But I was sure that the four men in those three boats would have completed their transactions long before then.

Strolling along the dock toward *Matata*, I wondered what contraband they might be dealing in tonight: cigarettes? Apparently there still was a lucrative trade in contraband—often counterfeit—American cigarettes all over the Mediterranean. They might be meeting a freighter at some rendezvous point to pick up a load of color televisions or videotape recorders. The heavy import duty on such luxury electronics made trafficking in television equipment an interesting business. Scotch whisky, of course, was still highly valued, especially in Muslim North Africa. Naturally, there were less wholesome possibilities. Each of those boats could carry a thousand pounds of Moroccan hashish in its closed forward compartment. If the contraband was morphine base or pure heroin, the weight would not have to be so large to turn a mammoth profit.

I stopped and listened to the last faint scratch of the boat's engines. Each one could also transport several cases of Uzzi submachine guns or Kalashnikov assault rifles or, perhaps, a dozen hand-held antiaircraft missiles. Increasingly that summer, the international press had reported suspected gun trafficking that involved the bartering of high-quality weapons for equally high-quality narcotics. Terrorist bands in the Middle East and Europe were, it seemed, involved in a strange criminal-commercial sequence. Italian Red Brigades cells, for example, might rob a Milan bank, use the proceeds of the robbery to buy heroin from the Sicilian Mafia, then trade the heroin to the Bulgarian state arms brokers for modern Soviet weapons and munitions. The Bulgarians would sell the dope for U.S. dollars in Europe. Weapons that were surplus to the terrorists' immediate needs might be peddled to fraternal terrorist bands, such as the Basque separatist ETA in Spain, the IRA in Ulster, or the Polisario in Spanish Sahara. All along the line, there were professional middlemen, such as the four young thugs in the speedboats that had just roared away to do some business out on the dark water of the strait.

The Mediterranean had long been a conduit for such irregular commerce, I realized. Both piracy and smuggling had been traditional avocations of most Mediterranean seafarers since the first men put to sea. The written history of the Med is replete with accounts of smuggling and piracy, ranging from the earliest Phoenicians up to the Barbary pirates on the shores of Tripoli. Looking at the large Mediterranean Sea Chart, it was easy to see that the Med was more of a natural trade route—connecting the Middle East with Western and Eastern Europe, North Africa, and the Atlantic—than it was a water barrier separating the different cultures that rose, flourished, and were extinguished along its shores. It was, in fact, the permeable nature of this sea boundary between Christian Europe and the Turkish Levant and Arab Barbary coast that encouraged so much cultural cross-fertilization—often carried out by smugglers—between the ostensibly mortal enemies in the Christian West and the Muslim East.

Just as Saracen princes relied on Genoese military architects to build their fortifications, and medieval Lombard dukes required Muslim cloves and coriander to spice their banquet platters, contemporary Moorish guerrillas in the Spanish Sahara used Bulgarian *Strela* missiles to shoot down Moroccan jets, and young people in squatter flats in Amsterdam and communes in Munich all smoked hashish and *kif* from the Maghreb, while trendy students in Fes and Marrakesh drank contraband Johnnie Walker Red. The various transient governments that have controlled the shores of the Mediterranean in the past five thousand years have tried, throughout those millennia, to "stamp out" nests of smugglers and pirates. Julius Caesar earned his military spurs as a young Roman patrician leading a punitive expedition against the Aegean pirates who had kidnapped him en route home from studying in Rhodes. Specialized, autonomous—ostensibly incorruptible—treasury and finance police organizations have swollen to bureaucratic ripeness all across the twentieth-century Mediterranean for the express purpose of *stamping out* smuggling.

Piracy per se has been abolished in the Med for a hundred years, although hijacking of valuable cargo from freighters, or from exposed smuggling operations, was still practiced around the Italian peninsula. And, unfortunately, the kidnapping for ransom of wealthy young people sailing the summer Mediterranean had recently become a subspecialty of the Sardinian Mafia. Apparently the Italian *Caribinieri* and navy were neither as efficient nor as ruthless as the young Ceasar; when he captured his former kidnappers, he reportedly sat them down to a final meal, then had them all crucified.

I wondered how many officials in Spain and Gibraltar the owner of the black cigarette boats had to bribe in order to maintain such brazen free access to port facilities here. I had spent the early part of my Foreign Service career in Africa idolizing the British colonial administration, which was, by comparison to the French and Belgian colonial governments of the countries where I served, a paradigm of just, incorruptible efficiency. After a few years, though, I came to realize that despite the panoply of auditors and inspectors general, the British colonial administration was also vulnerable to corruption. Here in Gibraltar, a British crown colony, the level of corruption was not pervasive, but surely *somebody* had to be on the take; otherwise those cigarette boats would not operate with such arrogant impunity.

I heard a whistling whine and looked up to see a lumbering RAF Shackleton bomber flare out for landing at the southern edge of the runway. The camouflaged plane looked like a prop from a World War II movie, until I noticed the bulging black electronics dome slung beneath the nose. This Shackleton was a long-range maritime patrol aircraft, keeping tabs on Soviet subs in the Med and far out on the Atlantic approaches to the strait. Powerful radars, magnetic sensors, and infrared scanners within that electronics dome could locate elusive nuclear submarines. Such devices could also undoubtedly pinpoint the three smuggling boats. But I did not think that the Royal Air Force bothered with such small fry. In the dangerous contest of the NATO-Warsaw Pact power struggle, cigarette boats—even those transshipping Soviet Kalashnikovs and plastic explosives en route to the IRA and Rote Armée Fraktion—were considered minor irritants.

Probably, I guessed, as I pulled up *Matata*'s stern warps to jump on board, their Lords of the Air Ministry, like their Lords of the Admiralty before them, realized the utter futility of attempting to stamp out smuggling in the Middle Sea.

I WAS SCRUBBING our laundry in the big tubs provided by the marina, bent over the ridged board and grumbling about the hard life of a sailor. Malcolm had gone to the harbor master's office to check for mail again. Around me several other women and a few men were at various stages in the soak-scrub-rinse process. Fervently, I thought, I'd pay anything for the use of an automatic washer. As I wrung the last pair of jeans through the old-fashioned hand roller, I paused; I didn't have *anything* to pay with, not yet. Mom, as usual, would come through with some money, but it was damn annoying that the royalty check wasn't here all the same. Today was Mal's birthday and unless there was a miracle we would not be going out to eat as was customary on both our birthdays.

I looked up as the thin young woman across from me swatted a child, hers I presumed, who was pulling at her as she scrubbed an old gray shirt on the wash board. "Jimmy, you can bloody well help me," she snarled. The little boy, not more than five I guessed, cringed and lowered his head, then crept up to the big tub. Right then I decided to stop maundering and feeling sorry for myself. I had chosen to make this trip as much as Malcolm had, knowing well the risk that it would have to be done on a tight budget. That child hadn't had any such choice. After a few days here in Gibraltar, I was amazed at how many people living on these boats had small children. Nobody seemed very well off either, and there was a grubbiness about both the boats and the people that was very unappealing. I was already looking forward to heading east.

Malcolm was waving a piece of paper in the air as he strode up the pier. "Doug's going to join us after all," he said. I heard the upbeat note in his voice. Doug had been one of Mal's students in creative writing at St. Lawrence University. During the Christmas semester break we had escaped from the bleak upstate New York winter by taking a group of ten students to the Virgin Islands to sail and study. The course was designed to teach seamanship as well as "Literature of the Sea." The mini-semester had been a success, for us and the students, and we'd gotten to know Doug well. He was intelligent and quiet, a good and trustworthy sailor. When we'd invited him to join us for some part of the trip, he hadn't been sure he could manage it. But he had.

Mal, I knew, would enjoy having someone else to talk to . . . more than that, someone to teach. He and I had, in the past few months especially, pretty well exchanged views on every possible subject, from how best to set the damn steering vane to critical analysis of Günter Grass's *The Flounder*. After nineteen years of marriage we had developed interests and skills that made us a good team, but there were times, like now, when an outsider added spice to our exotic stew of a life together.

The teacher in Malcolm would especially welcome a fresh student. And I would be glad of the extra, willing hands. In particular, another set of eyes to share watches now that we would be in the confines of the Med would be very important. As we island hopped from Gibraltar to Rhodes, there would be a lot of shipping and a much higher incidence of fishing fleets to keep a watch for, especially at night, than there had been in the open Atlantic. Our normal procedure of three hours on and three off with a third person sharing the duty meant each of us could have a *full six hours* of sack time—baring landfalls, near-collisions, sail changes, sudden squalls, etc. The expectation of that much

uninterrupted sleep was no small consideration in inviting Doug
to share our voyage. Although we had been in the marina here,
and before that in Tangier harbor, sleeping through the night for
over a week now, I vividly remembered those cold, brutal
awakenings at sea, after I had *just* fallen asleep. "Your watch,
Honey" . . . "Honey" to soften the blow. Being called even five
minutes early could build up a surprising amount of resentment.
Only when there was danger . . . "Carol a ship. I need you up
here" . . . was it easy to swing out of my bunk, feeling my way
in the dark back to the companionway to see whether I had time
to put on oilskins or if the emergency was so immediate that I
had to go on deck in my night clothes.

"When and how does he arrive?" I asked.

Malcolm shook his head. "Doesn't say, just he'll join us in Gib
the eighteenth or nineteenth." Mal looked back over his shoulder
as if expecting Doug to walk up the pier.

As we lugged the heavy buckets of wet laundry back to the
boat, we tried to figure out how Doug would get here. With the
border closed between Spain and Gib, as far as we knew there
were only two other routes: direct flight from London or via
Morocco.

Doug hadn't shown up at dinnertime to celebrate Malcolm's
fortieth birthday. To compensate for not going out to dinner, we
had a simple meal but one we both liked—the old English staple
of "bangers and mash"—and more than sufficient wine to wash it
down. We joked about Mal's birthday present: he got to sail
across the Atlantic Ocean on his own boat; not everyone's dream,
but it had been his.

"Hello, *Matata*, anyone aboard?"

I stuck my head out the center hatch, already knowing that it
must be Doug. He'd made it. Malcolm grunted across from me
and pulled his sleeping bag over his eyes. My head spun and my
stomach lurched as I pulled a sweatshirt over my head and
rummaged for my jeans in the pile of clothes on the shelf above

my bunk. We had indeed had too much of that cheap Moroccan wine last night. A good thing we weren't sailing, I thought.

As Doug jumped on board, first kicking off his sneakers, I noted that he had only one soft bag with him, thank goodness, as *Matata* was bursting with provisions and redundant equipment. He flopped onto the cockpit bench, right at home. Although he had been traveling all night, Doug looked fresh and cheerful. His thin, pale face exuded trust as he shyly took in the array of gear lashed down on deck. He was shorter than Mal and thinner, but having sailed with Doug for three weeks in the Caribbean I knew he was strong and would be a great help on the foredeck when it came to changing sails in the bad weather I knew the Med would throw at us.

We kept our voices low as we talked, and I made some coffee and took it up to the cockpit. Mal hadn't surfaced yet. Briefly, I was embarrassed when I told Doug why. I worried that admitting to our having hangovers would hardly be conducive to Doug's faith in our sailing ability. Here we were, the "adults," in a condition familiar to every college kid, hung over *and* broke, and he was throwing his lot in with us. But I needn't have worried. Our underweight stone of maturity was evenly balanced by his chips of experience. We'd get along fine.

Doug had flown to Madrid, taken a train down to Algeciras, and then discovered he couldn't cross the border to Gibraltar, which he could *see* across the bay. This morning he'd boarded the hydrofoil to Tangier, transfered there to another one for Gibraltar, not even getting his passport stamped in Morocco. "They really made me run around," he said, shaking his head, but smiling broadly as if he'd enjoyed it.

I showed Doug his bunk, the starboard quarterberth, and a locker where he could stow his things. While he unpacked, I'd rouse Malcolm, I said, unless he wanted to sleep?

Not Doug. "I'm ready to get started."

Just then, Malcolm burst through the connecting door to the main cabin. "Hey, Doug," he cried, grabbing his hand in welcome. "Boy, am I glad you could make it."

I had woken early and lay in my bunk, listening to the moan of jet engines at the RAF base nearby. Of course, in Gibraltar, everything was near to everything else; level land was at such a premium that the entire colony felt to me as if it had been originally laid out with normal distances prevailing between the airport and the marina, the dockyard and tourist hotels, the hospital and the power plant . . . then, somehow the jaws of some nightmare hydraulic press had compressed the entire settlement into its present cheek-by-jowl confines.

The barbed-wire and tank-trap barrier across the narrow causeway to the Spanish mainland only exacerbated this feeling of unnatural concentration. Gibraltar was like a ghetto that had outgrown its arbitrary boundaries and had turned in on itself with a malignant internal swelling.

Carol was still asleep opposite me in the portside bunk. Doug slept soundly in the starboard quarterberth. I heard a church bell sound seven times. Up in the cockpit, I listened to the British Forces news and weather forecast, then went to treat myself to a hot shower and shave. The lingering effects of another night of beer and wine produced a dull thickness in my head, reminding me that I was now, indeed, forty years old, that this was the twentieth of September, and that we had to sail soon or relinquish the dream of reaching Greece this year.

The telegraphic bank transfer had finally come through the day before, a fine birthday present. Unfortunately, the money had arrived too late in the day for us to cash the draft and enjoy a good restaurant meal. But that was just as well. Judging from Carol's careful budget calculations, we would have just enough cash to provision and fuel the boat and pay harbor fees on our trek across the Med.

But this budget did not include such items as charts, pilot books, or a dinghy. To secure the minimum necessary charts and pilots— we soon gave up the idea of a dinghy—we decided to sell off some "surplus" equipment we'd bought for the Atlantic crossing to people in the marina about to begin the tradewind passage to the Caribbean. We also hoped to swap our North American and Atlantic charts for those covering the Med with sailors outbound from Gib for points west.

So, after an early breakfast, I set out down the pier, lugging the spare compass, signal lamp, some surplus navigational gear, and rolled charts in a canvas bag, like an itinerant peddler. After a couple hours of displaying my wares and several embarrassingly intense bargaining sessions, I had managed to peddle a spare strobe light, a mayday signal balloon, and our reserve bulkhead compass. What was so frustrating was that the sailors I dealt with clearly were not able to offer anywhere near as much as the gear was worth. Like us, most of them seemed to be making their passages on shoestring budgets.

Others, with whom I sometimes came close to open acrimony, were live-aboards, permanently moored in the marina, who, like seasoned carrion birds, had sniffed out yet another broke passage maker and were interested in buying my gear for a pittance, probably for profitable resale later. My originally angry reaction, however, quickly gave way to the realization that these people were more to be pitied than held in contempt.

One older Englishman, in particular, seemed to epitomize the plight of these marina regulars. Like many of them, he was alone, living on a boat obviously too big for him to sail singlehanded. His was a rather chalky forty-foot fiber glass ketch of heavy displacement and mid-1960s design. The rigging was slack, the brightwork decidedly dull, and the running tackle a mess of greasy lines and loose, unwhipped ends. But his bar was well equipped, and he cajoled me into accepting a 9:00 A.M. Bloody Mary, so that he could replenish the small pitcher he had already started before I came aboard.

I'm not all that good at placing British accents, but I guessed his was Service, no doubt middle-grade officer. His tanned, stringy forearms were free of tattoos, his fingers bore no rings. He looked a boozy fifty.

The first thing he asked me, in theatrical *sotto voce*, casting a scowl in the direction of the marina office, was how much I'd been "stuck" for in dockage fees. When I told him that I'd negotiated a fee of thirty U.S. dollars a week, and five dollars a day for fractions thereof, he narrowed his eyes.

"Shocking," he said, as if actually shocked. "Management's *not* British, you know. Cypriot, I hear. Got themselves fixed up perfectly well with residency permits though. Could well be Jews. . . . " He gulped a mouthful of his drink, blinked at the hard sunlight in the companionway, and shook his head. "Sorry. You don't happen to be Jewish, I hope. One has to be sensitive to that type of thing with Americans . . . just a manner of speaking, isn't it? Jewish, I mean. . . . " He flourished his glass. "Sharp dealing, not really ethical, that's the notion I was trying to convey."

I explained that I was Irish-American on both sides, with a fair admixture of Scots-Irish.

My host took this information under silent advisement, then swung into an incongruous tirade against the British Inland Revenue and British tax codes, and the "bloody-minded socialists" in the Parliament. This unholy alliance had, according to him, made *droves* of his friends virtual exiles. They were, he assured me, honorably retired service officers and civil servants whose pensions went absolutely nowhere at home. They had opted for expatriate life abroad, here in the sunshine of the Med, aboard yachts or in *apartementos* ashore. Now, he added, the cowardly submission of the West to the blackmailing Arab oil cartel had sparked a global inflation that was rapidly making it impossible for them to live in places like Gib or the Costa del Sol. But, of course, if they did set foot in the U.K. for more than a few months each year, they'd forfeit their overseas resident status and thus become subject to "draconian" British taxes.

"It was our *dream*, you know," he continued, not bothering to identify the other person in the plural pronoun, "to have this boat, to cruise wherever struck our fancy. Seemed a damn fine plan at the time. Now . . . "

I remained silent, adopting what I hoped was a suitably commiserative expression. After a refill of our glasses, he pawed through my canvas bag of wares. He made the gesture—which I immediately, but politely, declined—of offering me two quid for the strobe light. I thanked him for the drink, shook his cool, surprisingly strong hand, and went ashore.

Halfway down the pier, I saw him sitting in his cockpit, smiling up at the sunlit wall of the Rock, a fresh Bloody Mary cupped in two hands below-his chest, like a liturgical chalice.

Along the slipways, I was now able to recognize boats similar to his. Many had dark skirts of weed at the waterline from months of inactivity. Some boasted the blue ensigns of retired service officers. Others were cluttered with rusty motorbikes and Rube Goldberg shopping carts; several had washlines and television antennae cluttering their rigging. What I was looking at, I came to realize, was a strange refugee camp, a transient center for displaced persons.

The Happy Ending leisure-time retirement explosion that brought forth the massive houseboats and fuel-hungry Winnebago campers in Sunbelt America in the 1960s had engendered a similar phenomenon in Europe's "sunbelt," the Mediterranean. But now the "blackmailing" oil merchants had, indeed, put an end to the dreams of many retired middle-class British. Stagflation, the truly frightening economic bogeyman of the 1970s, had hit marinas, seaside villas, and expatriate apartment blocks all the way from the Portuguese Algarve to Cyprus. Inflation undercut the small but dependable pension check; and Great Britain's stagnant economy precluded any meaningful dividend income from most pensioners' modest stock investments. Now they lived aboard their immobile yachts or in the *apartemento* barracks, victims of political and economic forces far removed from their influence or understanding. They shopped frugally, filling dull hours in the narrow lanes of the ubiquitous Mediterranean supermarkets that had mushroomed in every seaside resort community, carefully choosing *this* tin of tuna, and *that* brand of tea biscuit, as shrewd as refugee mothers in the market stalls along the Mekong opposite Vietianne, or in the flyblown *bidonvilles* of Nouakchott or Bamako.

The boat tied up at the end of the destroyer pen was named *Sarga*. She was a trim little oak double-ender with alloy spars, a wine-red mainsail neatly furled on her boom, and a well-varnished QME self-steering windvane on her stern.

On board, she was spotless, not glittery new like some of the French and German fiber glass sloops in the marina, but obviously maintained by people who knew boats well and who loved this one abidingly. Josh and Sarah were in their late twenties, sandy-haired, blue-eyed English, soft-spoken and relaxed. I guessed that they belonged to that post-1960s working class group of expatriates who had turned their backs on the narrow-minded monotony and permanently abrasive economic crisis of Britain and sought their fortunes abroad.

Josh was tall, over six feet. His long hands were calloused, and there was a permanent deposit of engine grease beneath his carefully pared fingernails. He made his living working on other people's boats: rigging, woodwork, mechanical repairs of all kinds.

Sarah was lithe but full-busted, deeply tanned. She could have been fashion-model material if she'd opted for that career. When I saw the scars and callouses on her wiry fingers, though, I realized that she took her job as an itinerant sailmaker seriously.

They were about to sail for Dakar and the start of an early trade-wind passage to Antigua and the Caribbean. The year before, they'd cruised *Sarga* the length of the Med and had wintered in Turkey, where they'd worked maintaining one of the new bareboat charter flotillas. Josh showed me around the boat, proudly indicating the pieces of rigging and equipment he'd salvaged from wrecks and abandoned hulks and adapted for service aboard their boat. They did not have an inboard engine, but the British Seagull, shining with a new black paint job and re-chromed flywheel, met their needs for auxiliary power. Josh had resurrected it from a machine-shop junk heap in an Italian boatyard. Their running lamps were kerosene and had come from an abandoned passenger tender he'd discovered rotting in a backwater creek in Malta. His plan was, he said, to make *Sarga* as autonomous, as nearly independent of ships' chandlers and shore resources as possible.

Their electrical power came from a small windmill generator mounted on the backstay. This charged a refurbished truck battery that, in turn, powered Sarah's sewing machine, which Josh had rigged with a twelve-volt motor.

Down in the cool main cabin, I noticed the gimbaled pine racks of mason jars that ran the length of the compartment above each settee. Sarah reached up and retrieved one of the quart jars to show me. "French beans," she said with quiet pride. "We stopped in Barcelona at the end of June, when the market was chock-a-block with vegetables. I put up enough beans and courgettes to last us the entire passage."

She'd also preserved homemade stew, barley soup, ratatouille, and tangerine marmalade. I was a little skeptical about the utility of those glass mason jars in a rough seaway, but Josh showed me how secure they were in the varnished wooden racks he had built without benefit of plans or power tools.

Over coffee, I spread out my Atlantic, Caribbean, and East Coast charts for their inspection. We quickly agreed that we'd swap charts one-for-one, and that a sheet of four or five harbor plans would be worth one-and-a-half large-scale area charts. After about forty minutes of flopping wide chart sheets on their small, gimbaled saloon table, we were all satisfied. They had obtained two broad Atlantic Ocean sheets that covered their route all the way from West Africa to the Caribbean, several charts of the Windward and Leeward islands, a number of individual island charts and harbor plans, and a full set of East Coast charts, all the way from Puerto Rico to Maine. In return, *Matata* had acquired seventeen nicely engraved British Admiralty charts that would take us safely from Gibraltar all the way to Greece. We already had on board several detailed Aegean charts from our previous sailing there, so I felt that, with a few additions from the local chandler, we'd have an adequate range of charts.

I swapped our Admiralty Atlantic and Caribbean pilot for their Mediterranean Pilot and List of Lights. My lower-latitude plotting sheets went for their catalogue of Mediterranean radio beacons.

By the time I clambered up to the hot concrete lip of the destroyer pen, I had in my canvas bag over two hundred dollars' worth of charts and pilot books, but I had not yet spent a penny of the $170 I'd earned selling surplus equipment earlier that day.

From the head of the pens, I looked back at *Sarga*, a pretty little ocean-going ship, nestled between two larger but less seaworthy plastic sloops. My thoughts reflexively returned to my bitter British host of that morning. He was, I realized, about to become extinct, just as inevitably as a dinosaur or any other of the planet's species that had failed to adapt to a drastically altered environment. When all was said and done, he was not a creature of the sea, despite the fact that he had chosen the sea on which to live. Ultimately, he needed the land; he depended on money that came from a complex and unpredictable economic web a thousand miles away to buy his eggs and bacon, his vodka and those expensive tins of Bloody Mary mix.

But Josh and Sarah, I knew, would no doubt realize their goal of sailing *Sarga* around the world. A winter season repairing engines and sewing sails in the Caribbean would replenish their cash supply. Then they would enter the Pacific via the Panama Canal and make the obligatory pilgrimage to the Galapagos and reach across the southeast trades to Polynesia—the "many islands" of the warm South Seas. Sarah would preserve their food in her gleaming mason jars; Josh would catch bonito and yellow fin and dry thin strips of filet. They would work hard for their money and husband it. Their personal discipline and ambitions were unconnected to the daily anxieties of currency exchange rates and stock market reports. They had opted out of the twentieth century and all its inherent complexities. They were young and healthy and possessed an unshakable—but clearly humorless—determination to accomplish their dream. In a way, they were hard-eyed pioneers.

Seated at *Sarga*'s teak saloon table, I had caught myself entering into the seduction of their dream, beginning to drift with the longing that, somehow, Carol and I could just cut loose, finally, irrevocably from the hassles of middle-class life . . . that we could sail *Matata* out the far end of the Med through the Suez Canal and down to the sandy lagoons of the South Pacific, that we could learn to live off the sea and find work among the colonies of boat people as had Josh and Sarah.

Out here in the noisy sunshine of Gibraltar's dockyard, however, I had to face the reality that Carol and I would never be content with such a truncated life. As attractive, as open and friendly as those two young people were, I knew they were ultimately shallow. Their knowledge of and interest in the world did not range much further than the confines of their boat or the port in which they were moored. Neither read the newspaper or listened to BBC news broadcasts; nor did they have any historical perspective of the countries and cultures in which they had lived or which they would visit in the coming years. They had carried with them their incurious working-class blandness to this radically different environment just as surely as the drunken retired officer had brought his own class's disappointed prejudices to that chalky white ketch.

I slung my canvas bag across my back and sauntered out the crumbling stucco gates of the dockyard. One problem with Carol and me, I now saw, was that we had acquired a taste for the luxurious freedom of the upper classes back during the expansive prosperity of the late sixties. We had grown used to the idea of a house and boat in Greece to which we would fly to spend part of each year, writing in the unspoiled tranquillity of an island village and cruising uncrowded coves and anchorages of the Dodecanese. But we also required the intellectual stimuli of the city: films, occasionally the theater, and a regular round of good dinner conversation. None of that, of course, could be had scratching out a salvage-and-barter existence aboard a boat like *Sarga*.

We were far different people from the sour expat exile grinning over his morning glass of vodka or the tanned young couple shrewdly calculating the price curves of eggplant and zucchini in Spanish markets. There was, I knew, a middle ground for us, one on which we could make our own living by writing and teaching and find a balance that would give us the time we needed to sail across the planet at our own pace.

High up on the Rock I saw the black specks of hawks, spiraling on the thermals rising from the hot limestone. I could not be certain, but I guessed those hawks were the same small reddish-brown falcons that I'd often watched gliding on the thermals above the cliffs of Lindos. I slung my sack higher on my shoulder, suddenly homesick for Greece and eager to be on our way across the Middle Sea.

CHAPTER THREE

LOG ENTRY FOR SEPTEMBER 22, 1979
GIBRALTAR TO PUERTO JOSÉ BANUS
ETD 1100   LOG 10.5
ETA 1700   LOG 40.0
TOTAL DISTANCE: 29.5 N.M.
BAR.: 30.75
SKY: STRAT/CIR-STRAT TO W/SW
WIND: BACKED TO S, FORCE 7 (35 KNOTS)
SEA: ROUGH, 6-8 FEET
COURSE: 40° TRUE

WE ROUNDED EUROPA POINT at 1130 and set course for José Banus. This port wasn't on our large-scale chart, but we had been told in Gib that there was a new marina there and that it was preferrable to the public one at Marbella a few miles up the coast. Mal and I thought we'd break Doug in easy and just have a short trip this first day, a couple of hours' sail to Spain. From José Banus we would visit Marbella, a typical Costa del Sol town. But by noon, as I tried to prepare lunch in our minuscule galley, the wind was increasing and it had swung south on us. We were beginning to dip and roll down some pretty steep waves. Doug looked like he was trying hard to keep a smile on his face. "Not hungry," he said to my offer of a sandwich. I have to admit that after lurching around below deck trying to put together a simple lunch for almost half an hour, I was feeling less than hungry. Malcolm, at the tiller, ate his sandwich and drank a beer, but I noticed he had a scowl on his face as he scanned the sea.

"Sorry," he said, obviously aware of how bad Doug and I were feeling from the look of us, "but we're going to have to change the jib."

Normally, I can handle almost anything at sea, but this particular motion—a kind of corkscrew with a slap and dip at the bottom of the trough—always got to me. Out in the Atlantic we would simply have altered course to have an easier ride, but that wasn't possible here in the relatively confined waters of the Mediterranean. Anyway, it would only be for a few hours, I told myself. It wasn't as if we had to keep going for days.

While I took over the helm, holding the boat as steady as I could, Mal and Doug went forward. They practically crawled on the pitching deck, clipping and unclipping their safety harnesses as they went. We had started out with one reef and the genoa, an appropriate balance of sails for a force five or six, which had been the forecast when we left Gib. That's what it had begun as too, but now we had a force seven with some very strong gusts, and the wind was almost directly behind us. The genoa had to come down and the working jib go up. Mal gave me a wave, pointing upwind, and I swung the bow around, pulling in the main sheet as I did so. The men had to scrabble on the wet and slippery deck to keep the dropping genny from landing in the water. It seemed to take forever as they bagged the sail and hanked on the smaller jib, while the boat rode up and over each swell on a beam reach. I knew that with a slight miscalculation on my part, however, we'd have green water over the deck, and, even on a warm day like this, Mal would not thank me for an impromptu bath. Doug had yet to be christened.

All that concentration and expended energy brought my stomach down to where it belonged. Besides, we now had a much easier ride, although still a tad too much sail. Doug brightened considerably. "I'll take that sandwich now," he said. "I guess I worked up an appetite."

Glancing back, I could see why the ancient Greeks had called the mountains guarding the mouth of the strait the Pillars of Hercules. The slight haze cut off the bottoms of both the Rock of Gibraltar (Djebel Tarik) and Djebel Moussa on the Moroccan coast. Indeed, from this perspective, those steep, high mountains looked very much like pillars framing the narrow neck of the entrance. Beyond was the unknown. Where we were, inside the bottle, was water that had been familiar to sailors as long ago as the Phoenician voyages of discovery and colonization in the eighth century B.C.

Malcolm was looking back too. In response to my comment about the fear the ancient mariners must have felt about the unknown that lay beyond the strait, he pointed out that you could fear the known as well. We both laughed weakly; we'd had our moments of fear crossing the Atlantic.

At 1530 we had to put in another reef. Spume was flying off the crests and we were dashing too fast down the steep waves. *Matata* was getting difficult to rein in. I had a look through the charts Mal had traded ours for back in Gib, but there was nothing small scale for this bit of coast. We were having a real problem now trying to find José Banus on that haze-shrouded coast, but Marbella stood out as a white smear to the northeast. If we had to, I knew, we could go into the public marina in the town, but the timing would be bad because we couldn't make it before dark.

I scanned the low land ahead with the glasses while trying to compensate for each swoop of the boat. It was no good; the dancing coastline was a featureless blur at this distance. We'd have to get in closer.

"I just can't make it out," I said, sitting down with a bump in the cockpit.

Malcolm took the glasses and looked too, but had to agree. "We're not really very far off," he said slowly, "but this is a lee shore and . . . I don't like it."

I didn't either. His concern was catching. I decided I had better go down to the chart table and work out a new course for Marbella, when I saw another sailboat, reaching down the coast. When the boat suddenly disappeared, I guessed it had passed behind the sea wall at the harbor entrance to José Banus. Now a gray, blockish mole separated itself from the shoreline. I could see waves crashing against it, sending up long white plumes of spray. I quickly took a bearing and Doug, on the helm, altered course. This had better be it, I thought. We had to go right in that entrance or risk a pounding on that sea wall.

At 1630 we were still searching for that elusive hole through which the other yacht had disappeared. *Matata* careened down the steep waves now, throwing us in spastic jerks toward the coast. Then a fast-moving cabin cruiser squirted out of the mouth of the harbor and we had our target pin-pointed. By now, with the shallow sea and the waves bunching up against the shore, the crazy swoops we were experiencing made manhandling the sails down more than any of us wanted to attempt. So, with the engine running, ready to let the sheets fly, we ran in the entrance, made a jog to port of ninety degrees—madly pulling in the sails—then tacked right around in a U-turn and ended up on a starboard beam reach in the calm water of the inner arm of the U. Catching our breath, we grinned at each other with relief as we slowly motored into the basin to drop our sails.

All the first ranks of docks were packed with large power boats, many flying the flags of the newly rich Arab countries on the Persian Gulf. Uniformed crews were washing, scrubbing, polishing, and immodestly showing off on almost every one of

these ostentatious small ships. The next group of boats were large
motor-sailers, with a few good-sized sailboats mixed in. Way at
the end, after some seven or eight docks, was a less formidable
looking array of boats our size. More like it!

For all the fancy dress of boutiques and modern cafés, the
marina fees were within our budget. And, after the scroungy,
well-worn public marina at Gibraltar, José Banus was a treat. The
wooden docks were still yellow-new. Flowers planted in neat
pine boxes placed every few meters lent the docks a festive,
colorful air. When I stepped ashore to tie us up, my bare feet
stayed clean instead of picking up the usual grease and dirt.

There was no town per se; the artificial harbor and marina
complex had created its own "town," including grocery stores
and restaurants, a hotel and several condominiums. That evening
we dressed up in our best shore clothes and strolled among the
attractive, well-groomed crowd on the waterfront. Most of them
were not "sailors" as we knew the type, but people who owned
yachts as luxurious appendages of themselves, like the chunky
gold jewelry they were all wearing that season. It was for show
but hardly useful. I'm sure not one of those people sitting at the
glass-and-chrome outdoor tables, sipping tall glasses of icy sangria,
had crossed the Atlantic on his own boat or even planned to go
as far as St. Tropez. The *crew* sailed the boat; owners jetted from
Marbella to St. Tropez, and then had a day cruise with friends
. . . if the sea wasn't too rough.

Possibly there were a few other people like ourselves who had
wandered into this haven for the rich, but they weren't out
strolling that night; nor did I see anyone who resembled a true
sailor the next day when I visited the fancy market shops. The
hands were the biggest giveaway. No one could sail a boat and
have those soft palms and polished nails; callouses and little nicks
and scratches came with the job.

This may have been a playground for the rich, but the prices
were very reasonable. For once I longed to stay an extra day
instead of getting under way as soon as our chores were done.
So, when Malcolm came back from the chandler to report that it

was closed until Monday and he couldn't get the small scale chart we needed until then, I was in favor of staying over an extra day. Doug seconded my motion, and Malcolm admitted that he, too, was enjoying this unaccustomed luxury. Besides, it gave us a chance to visit Marbella.

We flagged down the taxi just past the junction of the marina drive and the coastal highway. The car was a shining new Seat four-door, driven by a neatly dressed man of about fifty who sported a pencil-line mustache. Doug climbed in front, and Carol and I took the back seat.

"*Vamos a Marbella,*" I managed in my fractured high-school Spanish.

"*Muy bien,*" the driver responded, flipped on his left signal blinker, then pulled back onto the highway.

I caught a waft of cloying floral aftershave and noticed the rectangular scrap of a religious announcement pinned to the driver's sun visor. Bordered in black ink, the announcement featured a thick black cross in the center and a block of dense print: a memorial mass had been celebrated this morning for a Señora Maria Pilar . . . I could not distinguish the rest of the lady's five-barreled name. Since the driver wore no black arm band, I assumed the woman was neither his mother nor his wife. For some reason, this traditional religious trivium had a calming effect on me, a reassertion of the true Spanish ethos after the glittery comfort of José Banus.

The highway followed the flat coast north, passing olive and citrus groves and a couple of attractive *fincas.* But soon the view toward Marbella was dominated by a concrete ridgeline of recently built hotels and the ubiquitous *apartementos.* Ten years earlier, when we often visited Marbella from Tangier, the shore had been free of this oppressively monotonous tourist development. Then, the accepted myth among knowledgeable expats was that Marbella had been spared the urban sprawl of Torremolinos and Estepona because its *fincas* and villas were owned by influential officials in the Franco regime and by wealthy European jetsetters who had managed to reserve this section of the Costa del Sol for their exclusive use and protect it from the blight of shoddy highrises that was spreading from Gibraltar to Malaga.

Certainly the José Banus marina complex fit the image of an exclusive preserve of the upper classes. But the monolithic concrete barracks of *apartemento* complexes that marched across treeless, rubbly fields to the nearby beaches reminded me of housing projects in the Bronx. Between the soulless cement blocks, the sea looked gray and oily.

"*Not* very pretty," Carol muttered. She leaned forward and spoke to Doug. "This used to be such a nice stretch of coast . . . orchards and olive trees, whitewashed farm houses with tile roofs. We spent New Year's sixty-eight at some friends' *finca* just up the road here. You can't even see it now from the road."

"Looks like Fort Lauderdale," Doug said, then flashed his ready smile. "Wonder where all the college girls are."

"More likely sunburnt grandmas from Hamburg," I said, "with beer-keg thighs."

"Grandmas have to have granddaughters,' Doug replied. "You gotta look on the bright side."

As he and Carol chatted about the long-lost days of the 1960s, when the dollar was strong and the coast unspoiled, I experienced a deep rush of nostalgia for that last year we had spent in Tangier. In retrospect, that period had taken on unrealistically idyllic coloration. There was a seemingly endless bloody war in Indochina, widespread civil strife in America, and open rebellion on the streets of Europe, but our small post-colonial backwater had remained untouched by the global violence and contention. We were all, it seemed, bright, young, privileged and attractive. Those of us involved with the American School, the Peace Corps, or the A.I.D. program were untroubled by the prevailing radical cant that tarred any American government employee abroad as a neo-imperialist. We were confident that we were on the right side, and we accepted the posh housing, servants, and other perquisites as natural adjuncts to the careers of foreign service we had chosen.

The New Year's weekend that separated the "light at the end of the tunnel" optimism of 1967 from the Tet offensive reality of 1968, we had driven our white Mustang up this highway, six of us crammed in the car, with our tuxedos and long dresses packed in bags on the roof rack and two cases of PX champagne balanced on our laps. We had the use of Wes and Betsy Fenhagen's *finca* just outside Marbella. On New Year's day we would roast a goose. Monday there would be a *tentita* festival at a nearby bull ranch. We even had a table reserved at a new discotheque near the Marbella Club. All the way from the Algeciras ferry landing, we had sung along with Richard Alleman's new cassette recorder. The Beatles. . . . The magical mystery tour is waiting to take you away, take *us* away.

I was twenty-eight years old, Carol, twenty-six. The preserve of Andalucian tradition encompassing Marbella seemed a fitting locale for us to celebrate another passage in our expansive, untroubled young lives. I remember thinking with jejune but guileless arrogance that the domestic servants, waiters, and other Spaniards we encountered that weekend all had the calm dignity that is the touchstone of honest poverty. They were quaint, just like the whitewashed *fincas* and red-tile roofs. If they ever did become prosperous, I suspected, they would somehow lose their dignified simplicity.

The taxi neared the center of Marbella now, and stucco villas with shady gardens had replaced the garish blocks of highrises. I asked the driver to drop us off at the park that faced the cool, shadowy lanes of the Old Town. In that warren of narrow streets, I hoped that we could find a *tapas* bar that I remembered as being pure, uncompromising Andalucia.

Carol and Doug got out, and I leaned across the front seat to pay the fare, a few hundred peseta notes held loosely in my hand.

"*Siete centos,*" the driver said, watching my expression in his mirror.

Seven hundred pesetas was almost ten dollars, an outrageous amount to ask for a three-mile taxi ride. My face flushed with sudden, congested anger. There was certainly nothing quietly dignified about this bastard. "No, no," I blurted, "*siete centos es mucho . . . es muchicismo. . . .*" I didn't know the expression for "too much." ". . . *Excessivo,*" I finally offered in pidgin Spanish.

"*Siete centos no estan excessivimente, señor,*" the driver answered with bored disdain. "*Mira.*" He handed me a plastic-covered fare card that indicated in arcane dictionary syntax English that the "livery tariff" from the José Banus Marina to Marbella was double the kilometer rate, plus "attendance" charges. Now I saw what he was trying to pull. If people telephoned for a taxi from the marina, they naturally had to pay for a round trip. But we had flagged the driver down on the highway, not called to have him dispatched to that fancy damn marina.

I struggled to form the Spanish phrases of protest; I tried to relax and appeal to the man's reason, to demonstrate to him that we were *not* rich marks off some luxury yacht, but my languages suddenly became scrambled, and the words I found were French, Italian, and Greek. Finally I shook my head scornfully and shouted that I would "*lamar la policia . . .*"

Now the driver also lost his composure and launched into an incomprehensible diatribe that I believe concerned the former "fascist" government and the impotence of the police under the present democratic system. By this time, Doug and Carol were staring into the taxi with alarm, and passersby were gathering to watch the scene of potential violence from discrete vantage points on the palm-shaded sidewalk.

I released a clenched breath and shook my head with unfeigned bitterness. The unimpeachable honesty of the Spanish had always been one of the most attractive aspects of the country. I had traveled in Spain for twenty years and had never before been blatantly cheated. Digging in my wallet, I found four more hundred-peseta notes and dumped the seven bills onto the front seat.

Out on the sidewalk, Carol took my arm to slow my angry stride. "That wasn't very pleasant, was it?"

I glanced across the park to the encroaching highrise hotels. An air-conditioned bus of Scandinavians rumbled past. The breeze rustled in the dry palm fronds, and my pulse fluttered back to normal. "I guess you'd call that progress," I said as we started across the street, my relaxed, nostalgic Sunday ashore in Marbella indelibly tainted by the frustration and nastiness of the encounter.

In the cool side lanes of the Old Town, we stopped to admire the facades and window gardens. Obviously, the nearby *progress* of package tourist development had not yet penetrated here. A black-and-white cat carried a kitten in her mouth, swinging her small burden by the nape of its neck as she trotted down the worn cobbles and through a break in a garden wall. From outside the wall, we could hear the sweet, piping cries of her other kittens.

Deeper into the Old Town, we entered a small plaza, almost overgrown with roses and jasmine. Tangerine trees surrounded a Moorish fountain. We stopped in the scented shade and listened to the play of the water on the old tile. Andalucia had once been, of course, the heart of the world's most technically advanced and humane civilization for several centuries during the period we Western, Christian chauvanists have chosen to disparage as the Dark Ages. In Cordoba and Granada, doctors, poets, astronomers, bankers, and musicians congregated from places as far off as India and Damascus.

Sitting in the cool shadows, I wondered if the Swedish package tourists, or the dapper, dishonest taxi driver for that matter, knew anything about the court culture of the Moorish Caliphs. Probably not, I decided. The northern package tourists who frequented contemporary Andalucia sought sunshine, cheap alcohol, and unfettered sexual pleasure, not history. The middle-aged taxi driver would have spent his school years during the bloody trauma of the civil war; if the priests and nuns taught him, the Moors would probably have been dismissed as pagan interlopers on the sacred soil of Christian Spain. Education under the Republican administration, according to my Spanish friends, had been equally dogmatic: the Moors were seen as proto-imperialists in the long historical dialectic.

As we resumed our meandering pace, I mused on the ironies of mass tourism. During the two centuries that separate the Renaissance and the global wars of this century, tourism was the exclusive avocation of the privileged classes. Young nobles made grand tours to absorb classical culture. The new mercantile aristocracy of America aped this tradition and sent forth young people as disparate as Henry James and Mark Twain, who, despite their different perspectives, shared the accepted notion that tourism was a serious business: one traveled to become educated, to broaden, as the saying goes, one's horizons. Tourism in those days was also a reciprocal cultural exchange. Suitably upper-class local families often played host to the young traveler from northern Europe or America. In return, the young traveler was expected to be a worthy representative of his family and nation, to give the proper impression.

Naturally, the petit bourgeois and working people of that period did not indulge in international tourism. They stayed home and went about the grim business of survival.

Now, of course, tourism has become so radically transformed that it bears no resemblance to recreational travel in the past. Since the postwar economic boom, Europeans of all classes have embarked on annual migrations of biblical proportions. This flow of humanity has been almost exclusively from the prosperous, inclement north to the sunny, underdeveloped Mediterranean. In the process, entire urban areas, completely dependent on mass tourism—and now replete with street crime and inadequate sewage disposal—have mushroomed up to eradicate quiet fishing villages in Spain, Yugoslavia, and Greece. As during past migrations, there is often an invisible cultural confrontation in which the mores and language of the more prosperous invaders inevitably come to dominate the local people.

Blimpies and fish-and-chip stands have supplanted most of the *tapas* and *pinchitos* bars on the Costa del Sol. Multi-track Euro-rock —an unctuous, bland spinoff of the 1960s—now blares into white-washed lanes all across the summer Med. Indigenous guitar, mandolin, or bouzouki music seems about to become extinct. Margaritas and Scotch whisky are more popular than wine or *pastis*. English is the lingua franca of mass tourism from the Algarve to Jerusalem.

In a few years, the new culture is no longer foreign in these resort areas. With the advent of the Common Market, this process was accelerated. Now young people from northern Europe are free to establish bars, discotheques and fast-food stands in Mediterranean tourist centers. Kids growing up in these resort areas no longer face guest-worker emigration to the northern factories on reaching maturity. They stay home and work in the local tourist *factory*—a bar, hotel, disco, or restaurant—and, in the process, they acquire the language and values of their customers.

This transfer of values naturally includes attitudes about sex. Many young women from Scandinavia, Germany, or Britain consider a brief affair—or several one-night stands, for that matter—with a handsome local boy an integral part of any successful Mediterranean vacation. The local boys are usually eager to assist in this matter, and sea-front cafés and discos in the tourists' Med have become sexually predatory and joyless meat markets, just like their counterparts in Liverpool and Gothenburg.

One natural offshoot of this shift in values is a fracturing of local marital patterns. Boys are now often hesitant to marry a local girl when there is a seemingly inexhaustible supply of willing tourists available. As marriage often involves a dowry system on which the financial security of the boy's extended family traditionally has depended, this adopted pattern of sexuality has caused considerable social upheaval.

To many Mediterranean women, tourist women are simply whores. In turn, many tourist women have been emotionally devastated when they are suddenly dumped by the Mediterranean lover of several summers, who has finally succumbed to family pressure and married the well-dowried local girl his elders have chosen for him. As in most of the human encounters connected with mass tourism, mutual incomprehension eventually triumphs, just as it had during our encounter with the crooked taxi driver.

We finally found the Café Corrida, down a cul-de-sac, behind a small, seemingly unused church. It was, indeed, the *tapas* bar we remembered from our last visit to Marbella. The outside was nondescript white stucco with peeling green louvered shutters, half-closed on the midday glare. Inside there was cool shade, varnished oak tables with marble tops, a zinc bar, and ceiling fans. The bar could have been a set for the umpteenth remake of *The Sun Also Rises*. Canaries sang in an intricate wicker cage; two old men in berets played dominoes, and a large family, dressed in bright Sunday clothes, were grouped around a long table, working their way through heaped platters of cold and hot seafood *tapas*.

As our eyes adjusted to the shadows, Doug took in the décor, the peeling *ferrida* posters, and the glass-fronted ice box that displayed the cold *tapas*. I cold see that the pale lavender piles of uncooked squid and the squiggly heap of raw baby eels had caught his attention. I ordered a whole variety of *tapas* and iced bottles of Cruza Blanca beer, then we sat back in our comfortable cane chairs to relax after a morning of mixed anger, disappointment, and pleasure.

Doug watched intently as the portly señora behind the bar dumped handfuls of eels into spattering hot olive oil. She cleaned the small squid expertly, with single twisting strokes of a clumsy-looking butcher knife. In turn, the squid went into a shallower pan of bubbling oil. While the hot *tapas* were cooking, she brought us saucers of raw clams, winkles, sardines, and two kinds of marinated anchovies. I realized that probably the only dish Doug recognized as *food* on the table was the larger plate of boiled shrimp. But even they retained their orange shells and heads. Clearly, this was not a seafood buffet at the Red Lobster off the Long Island Expressway.

Doug cleared his throat and shifted in his chair. "Have they got any . . . ah, sort of fried fish or something?"

Carol smiled and popped a winkle neatly into her mouth. She squeezed a lemon wedge over the clams. "Take a piece of bread," she advised, taking a chunk herself. "Use the bread to pick up an anchovy, and soak up some of the marinade. That's where the flavor is."

With obvious trepidation, buffered by equally obvious determination to join into the spirit of the day, Doug ate a thin strand of anchovy and a hunk of the crusty brown bread. "Kind of salty," he smiled. "But good."

Slowly, with the grim concentration of a bomb-disposal man, Doug worked his way through the assorted cold *tapas*, sampling each. I demonstrated the correct method of shelling the boiled shrimp, and after two trials he seemed to have mastered the technique. Once a shrimp had been shelled, of course, it looked reassuringly like a plump, nicely boiled shrimp at a Holiday Inn Sunday smorgasbord anywhere in America. I did notice, however, that Doug had discreetly covered the severed, wall-eyed shrimp heads with his paper napkin.

When the lady brought us our hot *calamaras* and eels, I asked her for another plate of shrimp for Doug, anticipating that the hot *tapas* might not be to his liking.

Doug squinted at the plate of eels, curled to a crispy bronze like thinly sliced onion rings. "How do they clean them?" he asked. "They're so small."

"They don't," Carol replied, crunching down on a dainty handful. "The hot oil takes care of . . . well, you just don't have to clean the baby ones."

He took an eel and held it about six inches from his face, twisting it slowly in his fingers. "You eat the *head*, and everything?"

"Yep," I answered, demonstrating the technique.

Doug gingerly placed the untouched eel beside the napkin-shrouded shrimp heads. "I'm getting kind of full."

Next, the landlady delivered a plate of steamed salt cod, garnished with dill. Three tiny forks accompanied the dish, and I tried a sliver. The fish was hot, free of oil and about as bland as a fish stick dinner in a county jail. "Try the fish," I urged Doug. "I think you'll like it."

He did. In short order, he had put away the whole plate of cod, and I signaled for another and three more beers.

While Carol and I did gluttonous justice to the other dishes, Doug fashioned a meal of the shrimp, cod, bread, and several saucers of red-skinned peanuts.

We drank more beer and watched two little boys stand on their tiptoes to play a fast, serious game of *fus bal* table soccer. The canaries sang, the old domino players dozed in their chairs. Overhead the ceiling fans spun slowly. Sunlight slanted through the shutters.

For the first time since our landfall in Portugal, two weeks before, I felt that we had truly entered the timeless, stark tranquillity of the traditional Mediterranean. My earlier pessimism about the cultural corrosion of mass tourism was tempered now. The civilizations of this Middle Sea, I realized, had always been hybrid composites of invaders and indigenous people. Mass tourism was simply the latest of multiple conquests throughout the centuries. But the core, the essence of the native culture survived intact, preserved in tranquil refuges like this room.

ON MONDAY MORNING, Malcolm reported back to Doug and me on board *Matata*: the chandler was all out of the coastal charts covering the stretch of coast from José Banus to Cabo de Palos, from which we would set course for Ibiza in the Balearic islands. So we set off with inadequate charts again, but at least there'd be no need to go ashore between Marbella and the Balearics. We *did* have detailed charts of Ibiza.

As we motored out of the harbor entrance, Doug raised the mainsail, but there wasn't a lick of wind. The blue-gray sea heaved slightly, but the surface was as smooth as butter. Compared to our arrival two days before, visibility was extraordinary. The horizon was a deep blue pen stroke defining our world. The coastal greens and browns outlined the scattered *fincas* of sprawling, whitewashed houses topped by bright red crowns.

Because there was no wind, we couldn't use the self-steering vane and the helmsman had to stay on the tiller throughout his watch. During the day we each steered for two and a half hours at a time, giving the offwatch crew five hours to do chores and rest. Our course was set from headland to cape and the hours passed slowly as the landmarks came into sight, the helmsman recorded them, and they fell away behind us. By mid-afternoon a haze had developed along the coast, making steering by landmarks more difficult. The day passed in a monotonous round of watches.

This coastal cape-hopping was greatly enlivened at night by the dense freighter traffic that was following the same route as we were. But there was slower, less predictable traffic. Fishing boats worked the shoals both inside and outside our track. After being awakened several times by Malcolm or Doug for help in identifying approaching lights of freighters or trawlers, I decided to remain on deck on my offwatch, dozing on the cushioned cockpit bench.

At noon the next day there was still no wind. We had been powering more than twenty-four hours, using a lot of fuel. Although we hadn't planned to stop again before Ibiza, I began scanning the chart for likely harbors where we could top off the tank. Besides being low on fuel, we hadn't been able to get ice at the fancy marina in José Banus—I suppose all the other yachts there had generators and refrigeration—and we liked to have cold beer and soda during the hot day. Almeria, a large, working-class city, was the likely candidate for an overnight stop and we could easily make it into the harbor before dark.

At six that night we poked into the marina but were told we had to take on fuel and ice on the fishing dock, around the mole, on the side of the harbor. Tying up at that quayside took a great deal of effort. The high, rough stone wall was greasy and spiked with protruding rusty bolts and old wire-wrapped tires. Fishing boats were squeezed in all around us. An old, bent man, stared at us sullenly when we asked him to take a line as we came alongside, and Doug had to jump ashore, nearly landing in the oily water. Even after we thought we were settled for the night, we were told to move twice. The contrast with spit-and-polish, super-polite José Banus couldn't have been greater.

But this was 1979. These fishermen and workers were feeling a sense of freedom and power that had been quashed for all the years of Franco's reign. As we walked around the port that night, the signs of union activity were obvious, from socialist graffiti on the walls to the small bands of dark, scowling men who gathered in the cafés. We definitely felt unwelcome, not just as Americans, although that was implicit in the sneering way we heard the men whisper *Americano*, but as foreigners with money. *Matata* was a *fancy* yacht in their eyes, using *their*, the workers', dock.

Mal and Doug had already lugged a jerry can of diesel fuel from across the street and filled the tank, so we could have sailed that night, but there was no ice or fresh bread until morning. We decided to put up with the cold stares and careless maneuvering around our boat and get some sleep.

Very early and very rudely we were awakened by a large, wooden-hulled fishing smack, dripping tarry gook all over our deck, banging us as it left the dock. I was on deck in two seconds, in the sweatshirt and jeans that I had prudently slept in.

I stared down the leering fishermen on the opposite boat as I wedged a fender between the hulls. "Doug, Mal, get up here," I shouted. Mal, of course, was already shouting and fuming as he bounded up the companionway. He knew as well as I did that these men could maneuver their boats in and out of the harbor as delicately and efficiently as airplane pilots . . . if they chose to.

As soon as *that* boat was off, leaving a souvenir scrape on our topsides, another descended on us. We definitely felt paranoid, like there was some not very subtle purpose behind this assault other than poor boat handling.

"Let's get the hell out of here," I heard Mal shout to Doug while I was down below quickly stowing sleeping bags.

"But the ice and bread . . . " I called up.

Before I could continue, Doug had leaped ashore. "I'll get the ice," he said, charging down the dock. Within minutes he was back pushing a wheelbarrow with three bars of dirty ice. While I chopped and stowed the chunks, Mal started the engine and doubled off the shore lines. But before Doug could get back from across the square with the fresh bread, another fishing boat attacked us and an angry-looking clot of men on shore was shouting at us. Malcolm and I went into action. He let go the lines and we pulled off the dock, just in time to avoid another banging. Doug stood on the edge of the dock, a round loaf of crusty dark bread in each hand, staring after us.

It was nearly an hour before space cleared at the dock and we could round up alongside for Doug to jump aboard. With great relief, we set course for Cabo de Gata, right into a rising northeast wind. It would have been comfortable, exhilarating sailing in any other direction, but once again we had to power into it.

The slog up the coast was similar to the day before, only with wind and more sea. We motor-sailed through that night and the next day . . . weaving in and out of coastal traffic and fishing grounds dense with trawlers setting and retrieving nets—some of them probably the same sullen fishermen we'd encountered in Almeria.

At night it was spooky to have so many lights around after the deep darkness of Atlantic nights. Soon after we passed Alicante on the second day, Mal took some bearings and we changed course, heading for the channel between Ibiza and Formentera. That evening, before I turned in, I studied the chart and the List of Lights carefully. We were leaving the Iberian peninsula; henceforth, our voyage would be a series of offshore passages and landfalls as we skipped from island to island across the Middle Sea.

CHAPTER FOUR

SEPTEMBER 28, 1979
IBIZA

T he cockpit sole was slick with salt dew, but I hated to wake Carol to give her the helm while I went down to put on my sea boots. She and Doug had taken the earlier watches while I enjoyed the luxury of four hours' uninterrupted sleep. Now Carol slept soundly on the starboard cockpit bench, wrapped in her yellow oilskin jacket against the damp chill of the windless night.

On the black line of the horizon, the lighthouse flashed slowly, four times, then went dead. Pink ghosts danced on my retinas. For fifteen minutes I had been staring with painful intensity at the group-flashing light ahead of us. I estimated that we were approximately eight miles southwest of Ibiza. Powering with mainsail and engine through the sluggish residual swell of yesterday's northeast blow, we were closing on the channel between Ibiza and Formentera at about 5 knots. At 2115, Doug had logged the flashing light on Vedra Island, off the western tip of Ibiza, bearing 345 degrees true. Carol had picked up the group-occulting light on Isla Ahoroados that marked the northern lip of the Ibiza-Formentera Channel at 2205. And, at 2300, I had seen the light on Puercos Islet marking the channel's southern boundary. Then, twenty minutes later, this new light had appeared.

Without question, we were approaching the narrow, shallow channel; the three lights off Ibiza were so distinctive that there could be no doubt about their position. My problem did not concern those lighthouses. It was this strange, group-flashing-four that stood out so brightly, fine on the bow, bearing 60 degrees magnetic, exactly on our heading for the center of the channel, that had me worried. According to our charts, there was not supposed to *be* any light there. But, unless I was hallucinating due to short sleep during the bumpy, three-hundred-mile slog from Almeria, there definitely was a lighthouse out there where, just as definitely, there should not have been one.

Ibiza and Formentera were the southernmost islands of the Balearics, and, like Mallorca and Menorca further north, they offered a reasonably clear approach with a steep bottom contour, but the coasts shoaled up close in, and every cape was studded with rocks and obstacles. Exact piloting—especially on a night approach—was therefore vitally important. During their earlier watches, both Doug and Carol had taken their piloting responsibilities very seriously, working out painstaking, accurate bearings on the islands' lighthouses as soon as they appeared on the horizon. When I had relieved Carol, we had let the boat steer itself for ten minutes on the main and wind vane while we studied the chart together and verified the identity of the lighthouses from the Mediterranean List of Lights we'd acquired in Gib.

Until twenty minutes earlier, I had not been concerned about the approach. Now my anxiety was mounting to an uncomfortable level. This worry was complex, as well. The two-day, three-night beat from Almeria, east northeast into a nasty northeast blow, had been hard on all of us. Along the Spanish mainland between Cabo de Gata and Cabo de Palos, the shipping had been dense. We had experienced several near-collisions during that second night: the first provoked by a fishing trawler cutting across our bows that forced us to turn to port, right into the path of a fast coastal tanker. All during that night, there'd been scary encounters with ships and trawlers, and none of us had gotten much sleep. The next afternoon, the wind had eventually dropped, just after it had swung north and freed up enough for us to sail, full-and-by on the port tack for Ibiza. For eight hours, we'd powered into the vestigial swell, the boat rolling and clattering so badly that decent sleep had again been impossible.

By the random bad luck of the watch rotation, it seemed that Carol had been especially shortchanged on sleep during this passage, and I'd hoped to be able to let her sleep all the way through the channel, right up to the entrance to Ibiza harbor. Now, I knew, I was going to have to wake her to help me sort out what the hell kind of strange light we had out there on the bow. There simply were too many rocks ahead of us in the black shoal water for me to take a chance on blundering on until I could get a better look at the uncharted group-flashing light.

Once more, I was made overly anxious by claustrophobia. Out in the open Atlantic, I'd become used to the feeling of virtually infinite sea room, of the freedom to choose any course we wanted without fear of a lee shore. Here in the Med, there was no such luxury: our planned route to Greece included landfalls on Ibiza, Sardinia, Sicily, Malta, and Crete, all islands guarded by shoal water and rocky obstacles. I only hoped that our future approaches and landfalls would occur in daylight and good weather. But I realized that, given the weather of the autumn Med, I had no cause for optimism.

Before I broke down and woke Carol, I decided to check the charts once more. After adjusting the engine throttle and struggling with the tiller lines of the wind vane, I got the boat to steer a reasonably straight northeast course by itself, then slipped down the companionway to the chart table. In the hot glare of the chart light, I studied both the large American loran sheet we'd used for the passage from Almeria and the smaller British Admiralty plan of Ibiza-Formentera. Neither showed a group-flashing-four lighthouse anywhere near the channel separating the islands.

I sank down on the end of the quarterberth and rested the damp elbows of my oilskins on the chart table. Without thinking, I lit a cigarette, took a couple drags, coughed loudly, and stubbed it out. My mouth tasted awful: too much coffee, not enough sleep. Again, I leaned forward and studied the detailed chart with the magnifying glass. No question about it: the safe, three-fathom center of the channel lay between the group-occulting light on Isla Ahoroados and the group-flashing-two on Puerecos Islet. There were dangerous shoals both north and south of the centerline between those lights. Dully, my eyes sore and crusty, I stared down at the fine engraving of the British chart. The engine thumped loudly beside me; the boat steered itself through the slow, dark swell toward the even darker land.

Fingering the thick paper of the British chart, I let my mind go numb with the mechanical rhythm of the engine and with the temporary languor of delayed decision. This chart, number 3276, was a beautiful piece of work. It represented the combined skills of master mariners and master draftsmen and engravers. Every hill, ridge, stream and valley on the two islands was rendered in sharp detail. Each submerged rock and obstacle was carefully noted. The lines of fathom soundings were plentiful, but not so numerous as to provoke confusion. Automatically scanning down the chart, I read the legend at the bottom.

Based on surveys going back to 1804, it had been published as a detailed plan by the Admiralty on July 8, 1902, when Rear Admiral Sir W.J.L. Wharton was the royal hydrographer. The chart had last been corrected in 1974, less than five years earlier, so I assumed it was completely accurate.

Such an assumption, I thought, was about as safe as anyone could make these days. During the almost two hundred years since the Napoleonic wars, the Mediterranean had been a British lake, just as it had been the *mare nostrum* of the Romans twenty centuries earlier. The Royal Navy had been challenged and very nearly defeated on several occasions during that long tenure but had always risen victorious in the end. Keeping the Middle Sea open to British commerce guaranteed the safety of Egypt, Suez, and the Empire. And success of this naval endeavor depended, in no small part, on the accuracy of British Admiralty charts. An admiral or commodore who could plot the location of every rock and shoal, the profile of every headland and the elevation of every inland summit, held a vast advantage over opponents less well informed.

The history of seafaring in the Mediterranean was replete with shipwrecks, most of them founderings on uncharted lee-shore shoals and rocks. The anecdotal records of the early Christian church list no fewer than *six* shipwrecks that Saint Paul survived, preaching the gospel in the eastern Mediterranean. It was not until the middle of the nineteenth century that accurate charts of the Med came into widespread general use by navies and merchantmen of most Mediterranean countries. Before then, such charts were considered state secrets. Now, of course, in the tense peace that marks the last quarter of this century, carefully surveyed charts are available to anyone who goes to sea.

In fact, I recognized that, without these readily available charts—the ultimate legacy of Britain's past naval superiority—very few yacht sailors would put to sea. We depended on our charts just as we trusted the labels on medicine bottles and the electric signals that safely regulated our road traffic.

Now, apparently, I was coming to the nautical equivalent of a dangerous intersection, and the traffic lights were stuck. Once more, I gazed down at the finely engraved numbers and coastlines on the chart. There was absolutely no way a third light could have just . . . *cropped up* in the middle of that narrow channel. It was equally impossible that we could be approaching another corner of the island; nowhere else in the entire archipelago was there a pattern of group-occulting light facing a ten-second group-flashing two.

Reluctantly, I climbed back to the cockpit, took the tiller, and bent to wake Carol. She mumbled softly, opened her eyes, closed them, and rolled onto her other side, as if momentarily troubled by a dream. Again, I shook her elbow, then kneaded her upper arm.

"Carol . . . come on, Honey, we've got a little problem."

Again she rose to the surface of her deep sleep but was once more dragged down.

"Sorry," I said, reaching down to shake her shoulder more firmly.

Sputtering, and babbling sleepy nonsense, she finally woke. "What time is it?" she asked, her voice flat with displeasure.

"It's not your watch yet," I reassured her. "But we've got a problem with this light out there."

"What light?" she asked in the same tone, shielding her eyes from the glow of our stern lamp.

Coaxing and cajoling, I managed to get her sitting up. Slowly, she kneaded her face and became fully aware of her surroundings. I gave her the helm and slipped below to make a mug of strong instant coffee, generously laced with Spanish brandy.

When she had drunk half the mug, she sat on the cockpit bench opposite me and studied the British chart with the red-lensed penlight. "Well . . . " she muttered, her voice languid with fatigue, "you're right. There's not supposed to be a third light there. Are you sure that's the channel?"

Patiently, I reviewed the stages of piloting I had followed before waking her. Doug's bearing on the Vedra Island light was accurate, as was hers on the light marking the northern edge of the channel. My own cross bearing on the Puercos Islet light seemed right on the money. I'd even done a quick, three-point running fix on the lights that produced a tight cocked-hat position fix on the chart, which, in turn jibed nicely with the radio compass bearing I'd taken on the Ibiza airport radio beacon.

Returning slowly to alert rationality, Carol listened, then nodded firmly in the weak orange glow of the compass light. "That light should *not* be there."

"Well, it *is*. What do you think we ought to do?"

Over the years sailing with Carol, and especially since we'd set out across the Atlantic almost three months before, I had come to trust her judgment in situations like this. She was prudent but not paralyzed by overly cautious indecision. Between the two of us, we usually came up with the right course of action.

Speaking with slow determination, she suggested that I hold the boat exactly on course at a steady speed and she would take another series of running fixes, based on multiple compass bearings on the two lights we *knew* marked the channel boundaries. If our fixes conformed to the chart, we could be certain of our position. Then, as we neared the strange flashing light, we would slow down and give it as wide a berth as possible, once we had verified the dimensions of the channel with binoculars. It was, I saw, the correct course to follow. Sitting on the portside bench, I reached down to adjust the throttle to two-thirds revs, then studied the compass as I steered smack on 60 degrees magnetic.

Within fifteen minutes, Carol had run her bearings and fixes and had confirmed our position, four miles due southwest of the channel center. She made more coffee and brought the brandy bottle up with her to set beside the two steaming mugs.

"Damn light's got to be marking some kind of a *wreck* or something," she muttered.

I was craning ahead again, staring over the cabintop. The bright flash of the light was dead on the bow. Slowly, with a wavering smear of dark on dark, I began to distinguish a vertical black mass just beneath the light. On either side, the two charted lighthouses pulsed silently in their appointed positions. The sea was flat and greasy this close in because the bulk of the island blocked the swell from the northeast. I had the impression suddenly that the flowing geometry of darkness and lights ahead of us was some kind of computer graphic, like the elaborate night-landing simlators used to train airline pilots.

Ten minutes later, I could clearly see the structure of a black metal-grid tower supporting the group-flashing light, right in the center of the channel. We slowed to about 3 knots and approached the channel entrance, leaving the tower fine on the port bow. As the strange structure slid toward us, I steered slightly south of course to let the tower glide past fifty yards on the port beam. Carol sipped her coffee, glaring at the uncharted light.

The satiny black thickness of the two capes drifted behind us, and, ahead to starboard, the lighthouse on Espardell Islet appeared right on its correct bearing. Carol leaned over the port cockpit coaming, searching with the binoculars to the northeast for the light on the Dado Grande Rock that marked the nasty Malvin shoals between us and Ibiza harbor. As soon as we had that light and the white-red occulting light at Isola Grossa, we could lay a safe course past the rocks and power right into the harbor.

I licked my dry lips, anticipating an icy Scotch and water, then a long sleep in the silky folds of my sleeping bag. It had been a troubling end of an uncomfortable passage, but now, I reassured myself, the trip was almost over.

Carol shook me awake and I found myself sputtering and groping about incoherently, just as she had two hours earlier.

"What's the time?" I automatically asked.

"Almost three," she said. "Call Doug, would you? We've got another problem with these damn lights."

I sat up so fast my vision danced with dizzy green worms. I'd been sleeping about an hour on the cockpit bench but still felt punchy from accumulated fatigue. After I called Doug—who moaned loudly but quickly pulled on his jeans and oilskins when I said we had a problem—I sloshed my face with cold water from the ice chest and choked down half a cup of tepid coffee.

Carol was steering north northeast, 30 degrees, still on the mainsail and engine. Off to port, the mass of the island rose from the dark sheen of the sea. I sat beside Carol and rubbed the last sleep from my eyes as I tried to get my bearings.

"Right back on the port quarter," Carol pointed, "that's the Dado Grande Rock light. From here we should be getting that red-and-white occulting. . . . " Her voice was thin with tired frustration. "The chart says it's got a range of ten miles."

I studied the chart with the penlight. She was right, of course. On this heading, with the Dado Grande light astern, we *had* to pick up the two-colored harbor entrance light on the port beam. Leaning closer to the damp sheet of the chart, I saw that our current course was taking us directly toward the unlit rocks of North and South Llado islets, two miles northeast of the harbor.

Inshore, the usual looping street-light necklaces of a sleeping town climbed the hillsides above the invisible harbor. To the southwest, an occasional airliner silently descended into the mountain shadow above the airport. I was awake now, and I understood the reason for

Carol's anxiety. The red-and-white light at Isla Grossa was our cross bearing; without it, we were still uncertain of our position as we blundered along blindly through this shoal water.

"I'll take it," I said, hoping my voice sounded reasonably calm.

I slowed the engine to one-third revs and turned to take another rough eyeball bearing on the Dado Grande light astern. "What time were we abeam that light?"

"About two, two-thirty," Carol said. She was pulling on her oil-skin trousers against the soaking dew that had beaded on every surface.

"No," I said, sudden irritation cutting into my tone. "I mean what time *exactly* did you log us passing that light?"

"I didn't *log* it," she said, her own anger showing now. "You were just going to sleep, and I didn't want to wake you. I figured we'd get the other light soon enough, anyway."

"God*damn* it." I gave vent now to my frustration. "We've got rocks right ahead of us. We . . . "

"Just wait a second," Carol interrupted. "We won't be near those two rocks until we pass the other light."

"Well, what the hell did you wake me up for if you're so positive?"

Carol glared at me but did not answer. Doug climbed into the cockpit and looked around him, blinking at the confusing array of city lights. "What's up?"

Carol shook her head. "Well . . . we had a light back in the channel that shouldn't have been there, and now we *don't* have a light that's supposed to be there."

My sudden, irrational anger had dissolved. "Look," I said, trying to speak reasonably, "let's go about, power down until we get good bearings on the Dado Grande light and that group-flashing three on Espardell Islet back there, check the log, then steer a good compass course northeast again for three miles or whatever, then turn north-west and head right in."

Carol sat with her head down, dejected and overtired. Silently, she nodded.

"I'll steer back to the light," Doug said. "You guys just relax."

I sat down on the squishy cockpit cushion, uncomfortably aware of my sodden jeans. Doug turned back to the reciprocal course of 240 degrees, and the dark mass of the island rotated through the night. Ahead of us, the yellow light on Dado Grande cast a shimmering yellow tail on the flat surface. When I closed my eyes, faint strobes and pinwheels exploded along my optic nerves. The night suddenly seemed palpably threatening, evil. I wanted the next two hours to be over; I wanted sleep; I wanted a stiff drink of Scotch and eight hours alone in my sleeping bag; this damn boat and this goddamned ill-advised trek forgotten.

As if reading my thoughts, Carol stretched and muttered something.

"What did you say, Honey?" I asked, uncertain of her exact words.

She drew herself upright and stared out at the dark water. "I said, 'I wonder why the hell they call these things *pleasure* boats.'"

At 0520, with the sky to the east beginning to pale with false dawn, we began our final, overly cautious approach on Ibiza harbor. About two thousand yards northeast, we could just distinguish the steel girder tower of the light on Isla Grossa. Through the binoculars, it was readily apparent that the light was not functioning. Carol took the glasses and confirmed this seemingly unacceptable fact; then Doug followed suit. The red-and-white occulting light for which we'd been searching for the previous three hours was dead.

But we did have the cape on Isla Grossa marked now, so we could get a wobbly cross bearing: enough to set a reasonably safe course from the Dado Grande light to the flashing red light at the western end of the Ibiza harbor sea wall, a course that had taken us within one hundred yards of several shallowly submerged rocks.

It was just before six when we rounded the mole and powered up the channel toward the Nueva Ibiza marina. Carol ducked below and poured three plastic tumblers of straight Scotch. We each drank with unusual, silent concentration, trying with mixed success to banish the tensions and frustrations of the night. But I believe that all three of us felt cheated, that a sacred trust had been broken by the problems with the two lighthouses, one that was uncharted and the other that had inexplicably been dead.

I also realized that the problems with the two lights might well have been covered in recent Notices to Mariners, but I knew that our hodgepodge collection of charts, light catalogues, and pilot books did not include such recently updated information. We still had two-thirds of our passage ahead of us. How many more such nasty surprises would there be?

We turned into the marina, a large, modern complex of concrete jetties and elaborate shore facilities.

Doug stood at the starboard shrouds hitching on a fender. "You know," he said with somber reflection in his voice, "these night landfalls are going to be a *lot* of trouble if we can't trust the damn charts."

Carol was bent over the cockpit bench, uncoiling a dock line. She rose and blinked at the bright street lamps lining the pier. "Out there," she said softly, echoing each of our thoughts, "it's so different. The night makes it all so, well . . . primitive, like the rocks were somehow waiting to get us. Did you feel that, or am I just paranoid?"

I nodded agreement, glancing with distaste at the darkness beyond the sea wall's boundary of civilization. Ahead of us, a Mediterranean resort community was beginning to awake for another day in the long season of organized hedonism. "I know exactly what you mean," I answered.

High above, a plume of cirrus caught the early sun, glowed peach, then took on the metallic pink of ripe apples. Comforting daylight had come to banish the primitive night.

NUEVA IBIZA
SEPTEMBER 29 TO OCTOBER 1

OUR MISSING-LIGHT and one-where-it-shouldn't-be introduction to this ancient port was only a sample of the bizarre experiences that were in store for us. Malcolm and I had been around Mediterranean tourist resorts for fifteen years, and Doug wasn't born yesterday, but Ibiza was a shock for us all.

When Mal and I lived in Tangier, Ibiza—although we'd never had a chance to go there—was often described as a tranquil, laid-back, artists' colony type of place, somewhere you'd spend a holiday when you wanted to escape from civilization. Artists— writers, painters, and poets—are renowned for finding the most attractive settings from Capri to Mykonos, with local color, decent food, and cheap drink. Ostensibly, Ibiza was such a place. But what happened to this "paradise" has happened to dozens of other resorts before; it was discovered. Local people first enlarged, then sold their houses and shops, and . . . in the process, they lost their character, their sense of communal pride. Soon, "real" artists couldn't afford to live there anymore and wouldn't want to if they could. They moved on, but their places were quickly taken by the ubiquitous group-charter tourists. With little interest in the cultural history of the place and caring even less about the local customs, they often offended the indigenous people in their continuing quest for the sun, especially by their casual nudity.

That first morning nothing seemed too odd; the marina berth we were assigned was quiet and convenient, offering hookups for electricity and water on each dock, free showers ashore, and other amenities. While I rinsed out a few towels in a bucket in the cockpit, Doug walked into town for the day. Malcolm finished washing down our deck then offered to help me.

"Why not go ask about those lights at the harbor master's office?" I suggested. Now that we were safely ensconced in the marina, the night's difficult approach to the harbor due to the two problem lights seemed less frightening than annoying.

I was bending over the bucket, squeezing out the last towel and rather enjoying the warm sun on my bare shoulders, when I heard a shout from an inflatable Zodiac cruising between the docks. "Welcome, *Matata.*" It was Willy and Gordon off *Mango.* We'd last met them in Horta almost a month ago. I don't remember which one was the skipper, as they seemed to share responsibility. They were delivering the big motor-sailer to Greece for the owner, all the way from British Columbia, and had been at sea for months. Not always on the water of course;

they seemed to take every opportunity to go ashore and enjoy themselves. But, despite their perennial joviality, it was easy to discern a wistful note of loneliness in their conversation. Making a living out of delivering boats to distant corners of the world was a hard and ultimately very lonely occupation. I guessed that they made up for the long watchkeeping hours alone on deck by cramming in as much partying as possible once they hit a port.

The work of crewing a large sailboat for long distances is physically hard, as Malcolm and I had discovered, but there is also a great deal of psychological strain. Our twenty-eight day crossing from New York to the Azores had brought this home to us. But sailing long distances was not our *life*; we could quit any time. Our reasons were different for undertaking such a voyage: we weren't doing it to make money, but rather for the experience. For Willy and Gordon, *Mango* wasn't even their boat. Soon the owner would meet them and pay them for their time. They would go on to the next job, another boat, a different passage. I couldn't imagine turning *Matata* over to someone else at the end of a voyage.

Malcolm soon reappeared and, after a beer aboard *Matata*, we all went in their dinghy to the public marina where *Mango* was moored. This marina was much closer to town and less modern but preferable for a couple of guys who wanted to check out the scene in Ibiza every afternoon and evening. We arranged to meet that night in town for a drink.

Malcolm and I strolled along the waterfront to explore Ibiza. At first the town seemed normal enough. The streets between the four-story stone buildings were crowded with ordinary Spanish women in dark, well-cut clothes, carrying their string bags full of oranges and brown-paper-wrapped sausages. Small groups of men clustered around tiny zinc-topped tables in the cafés, drinking and talking. There were a lot of Seats on the narrow streets, tooting their tinny horns. It was almost like a mainland city, industrious-looking and prosperous.

But, as we followed the road that skirted the inner harbor, we left the modern *puerto* behind and entered the old town of Ibiza.

The Balearic islands were originally settled by Phoenicians and Carthaginians, only to be conquered by the Romans in 123 B.C. Throughout the Mediterranean, these old village sites chosen by the classical mariners have a similar look and feel: they are almost all built on promontories, the buildings climbing the steeply sloping high ground above a safe anchorage. In a storm, shallow-draft ships could be drawn up on the sandy shore. The usual warren of narrow, crooked streets between blockish stone houses with enclosed courtyards was as familiar here as it was in Lindos or Tangier.

As we ambled side by side I glanced at Malcolm. His eyes were hidden by sunglasses, but I could tell from the set of his shoulders and the tightness around his lips that he was disapproving of something. He poked me, then took hold of my hand. In front of us, but strolling much slower, were a group of young foreigners—Germans, we discovered as we came abreast and heard them speaking. There were two girls and a boy. One girl wore light blue satiny shorts, but really *short*. They weren't meant for exercise or intended to cover her buttocks. Her feet were shod in high-heeled, pastel *cowboy* boots, reaching to mid-calf. Decidedly odd. As we came even, I slowed and nearly tripped. She had a see-through fishnet shirt draped across her front.

The other girl was similarly dressed, but not quite as flashy. And the boy was decked out in a *lavender* one-piece flight suit with shiny zippers marking superfluous pockets. He, too, wore garish cowboy boots. Now another young man joined this group. He flashed a wad of 1,000-peseta notes and grumbled over his shoulder. A shopkeeper sullenly stared from his doorway at the haughty, rich German. This young man's taste tended toward fake leopardskin. If I could have seen Mal's eyes, I'm sure he would have been rolling them in wonder.

"Did you see that wad?" he exclaimed as soon as we were out of earshot. "The guy in the spots must have had a thousand bucks in pesetas there."

I nodded. These were just *kids*, probably not more than twenty-one or twenty-two. They came from an endless free-lunch educational and welfare society of the north. They were probably computer programmers or electronics technicians, something well paid but dull. If they went to university, they not only attended tuition-free but received a generous living stipend. This postwar generation of young Germans exhibited their hedonistic lifestyle blatantly, not caring whether they offended others. All around us were shops and boutiques blaring out rock music to entice these visitors to buy. The piles of gaudy and cheap clothes were, no doubt, produced especially for the tastes of this crowd. This whole section of Ibiza had the atmosphere of ersatz Rodeo Drive, a slightly seedy fashion street built on glittery hedonism.

We were now in the old village center of Ibiza and it looked like a punk rock movie set. The few Spanish people in evidence seemed oblivious to their strange environment. Mostly waiters, they dashed from table to table in the outdoor cafés serving what we discovered were overpriced drinks on gummy, wet trays to these flamboyant creatures from the north. If anyone stood out in this crowd, it was Malcolm and me. We looked pretty straight in our jeans, T-shirts, and plain white sneakers, not a scrap of electric lavender on us.

We began to climb up through the cobbled streets, as if in search of some remnant of the past. If you concentrated you could still see what the town must have been like. There were flowers, red geraniums—the weed of the Mediterranean— everywhere. A few of the small, pretty houses that had not been converted into restaurants, boutiques, or rock music cassette shops actually served to shelter people, but everyone we saw was foreign, *not* Spanish. It was as if the local inhabitants had been banished beyond some invisible wall by this new group of colonists. Near the top of the promontory, we looked over a parapet and out to sea. Below, I could clearly see all the rocks we had spent the night avoiding as we tried to pick out our light. Even from this distance, they looked sharp and dangerous. Black patches were sinister evidence of underwater snares we would have trouble seeing even in daylight without some landmarks to steer by.

Mal was looking down too. He pointed out the light that was out of service. "The harbor master said, 'Oh *that* light; it's been out for a long time. You should not try to come in here at night.'" For a moment Mal was silent. "I think we should really avoid these night approaches in the future."

As we watched, a sailboat about the size of *Matata* rounded the islet where the useless light perched on its metal tower. The main was already set and we could see them harden up to raise the jib. Their course looked due east, the same as we would be taking tomorrow.

That evening, we found it entertaining, in a bitchy sort of way, to sit at a café table and observe the antics of the colorful flocks of wealthy migrants. This time it was my birthday, and we celebrated with a night out in Ibiza. Between the entree and the dessert course, we witnessed the spectacle of a fire-eater doing his tricks. I guessed he was Italian, but Doug and Mal insisted he was Spanish. Probably he was a gypsy and equally at home in any Mediterranean country. He started simply, lighting a cigarette and smoking it *inside* his mouth. Soon he moved on to bigger things; with his head back he poured kerosene down his throat, lit a match, then spewed out a four-foot sword of flame. Somehow he managed to do this without setting his long hair alight. A child of about eight years old, almost an exact replica of the fire-eater, passed among the spectators, a flat cap held upside-down to receive the contributions. We figured the whole crazy show was worth a few pesetas.

Later, when Doug treated us to a birthday nightcap at another café down a quiet cul-de-sac, we talked about our impressions of Ibiza.

"Weird," was Doug's basic pronouncement. "You'd think you were on Bleeker Street on a Saturday night."

Malcolm was more peremptory: "We can definitely cross this one off our list."

Indeed, I could see no reason to visit here again, but it had been what they call an enlightening experience.

As we walked back to the boat that night—we'd had a couple of drinks, but we certainly weren't drunk—a *very* strange green light flashed above our heads. Then again. It seemed to be some kind of dazzling, electric-lime laser beam, slowly revolving from a high point ahead of us. Soon we discovered its origin: a discotheque perched on a small cliff overlooking the marina. I assume the light was meant to lure customers, a beacon to mark their destination. Thank goodness it hadn't been flashing the night we made our approach to the harbor. That's all we would have needed.

CHAPTER FIVE

TAFFRAIL LOG: 284 MILES FROM IBIZA (CAPE CASTELLA)
WIND: E/SE 6 (28 KNOTS)
SEA: ROUGH (6-8 FEET), SHORT, NASTY SWELL
SKY: CIR-STRAT ACROSS NW SKY
BAR.: 30.72, FALLING FAST

Comments: Reefed main at 1030. Wind heading us and rising. A lot of spray.

C arol was waging one of her familiar battles in the galley, across from me, trying with mixed success to produce a lunch of hot soup and salami sandwiches without redecorating the bulkheads with split peas. The boat pounded and creaked. Hard spray clattered on the plexiglass hatches. I was jammed into the snug corner between the engine box and the chart table, doing my best to clean the sextant, which had received a salt-water shower while I was taking the noon sight for the meridian pass.

Naturally, the cabin was buttoned up tight against the spray, and it was stuffy and sick-making down here. The smell of food did not especially help my queasy stomach as I worked doggedly with a cotton swab to dry the small tracks and springs of the sextant. I was woozy from the effort of calculating, then plotting our noon position, the first complicated celestial navigation I'd done in three weeks.

The navigation had not been unpleasant, however. I still got an inordinant rush of joy when the abstract numbers of the sextant heights and the sterile columns of logarithms from the Sight Reduction Table actually rendered coordinates I could plot on the chart with absolute confidence that they represented our position on this huge spinning planet.

Our local noon position—39°41' North by 7°13' East—had worked out to be pretty close to our dead-reckoning estimate. That put us about seventy miles southwest of our landfall, Cape San Marco on the west coast of Sardinia. For the past three days, we'd had a mixed bag of weather and had resorted to powering into a light easterly breeze for most of the previous twenty-four hours. But that morning the breeze rose to a real wind and veered around about twenty degrees to the southeast. At 1030, Doug and I had reefed the mainsail and shortened down to the stout working jib. All morning, I'd watched the sky signs of a large depression building above the northwestern horizon. Around 1100, our own barometer began to drop, and I was convinced we were in for a blow.

After cleaning the sextant, I gamely attempted to find a weather report on short wave. The BBC World Service came in clearly on the higher frequency wave bands, but the lower frequencies were a noisy jumble of static—wailing *mullahs* and breathless Italian disc jockeys going overboard with the echo chamber. I made a show of consulting the salt-spattered Mediterranean Pilot we'd picked up in Gib but decided to wait a while before searching for the French maritime stations it listed.

I needed fresh air before I actually got seasick.

"Want any help?" I asked Carol with token sincerity, as I did my orangutan routine on the overhead grab rails and swung up to the companionway.

She smiled grimly and shook her head, one hand hovering above the wooden bowl of sandwiches while she stirred the soup sloshing around the pressure cooker wedged onto the swaying stove. Early in the trip, we had agreed to this division of labor: in rough weather, she was easily the more competent cook, and I the more proficient navigator. We weren't gender-chauvinistic about these chores at other times, but we each recognized our limitations, as well as the importance of these nautical skills. Hot, appetizing, and nourishing food was, of course, every bit as important to the well-being and ultimate safety of the crew as accurate navigation.

Leaving her to the acrobatics of preparing a meal, I slid back the hatch and scissored my way over the stormboards. Spray slapped my left cheek just as I was yanking up the hood of my oilskin jacket. Instinctively, I looked to windward. In the thirty minutes I'd been down below hassling with the plotting sheets, the wind had risen another 5 knots. The sea had also mounted, and the white crests that marched down on us from the southeast were acquiring that short, angular shape so typical of Mediterranean storm conditions.

In the Atlantic, a storm had thousands of miles of sea to develop its wave geometry. Here in the Med, the offshore reaches were much more restricted. The short, confused "pyramid" sea, as we used to call it in Greece, was the usual pattern when the wind got up above force six.

"How we doing?" I asked as I lurched onto the wet cockpit bench opposite Doug.

He was hunched over on the lowside, his yellow oilskin back to the bow. At the stern, the faithful plywood blade of the steering wind vane rocked and tilted with each gust, driving the web of faded red lines to the tiller to steer the boat east.

"Getting kind of bumpy," Doug said, nodding toward the tiller lines. "I had to put the shock cord on her."

When the gusts overpowered the compensating pressure of the

wind vane, we had to reinforce the weatherside tiller lines with an elastic shock cord. Normally, we didn't do this until there were puffs above 30 knots. And that was what we were now experiencing. I gingerly got to my feet, gripping the end of the boom and the cabintop to brace myself against the pounding. Aft, the entire western sky had now glazed over with a sour-milk blanket of cirro-stratus. Ahead, there was still blue sky and sunlight, but somehow the *summer* quality of the day had been irrevocably forfeited. I had the definite feeling that autumn was declaring itself, that, indeed, we were being formally introduced to the season of post-equinox storms that I had brooded about in Tangier and Gibraltar.

As if sensing my mood, Doug rose on his elbows again to stare at the confused seascape. "You get a decent weather forecast on the radio?" he asked.

"Nope," I muttered, sitting back down in the pitching cockpit. "But I don't think we need one to see what's happening today."

Carol rapped sharply on the closed hatch, and Doug sprang forward to help her with the bowls of food. Once she was settled in a dry corner of the cockpit and had done her deep-breathing routine to clear her head, we dug into our food. Naturally enough, today's lunch conversation concerned the nature of Mediterranean wind systems. Doug had grown up and had done most of his sailing in Long Island Sound and, like many American sailors, was unfamiliar with weather over here.

Carol and I first pointed out the vast difference in the geography of the Mediterranean's northern and southern shores—Eurasia and Africa—that surrounded this "middle sea." Europe's weather, like that of North America, was influenced by the Arctic jet streams and the depressions that formed in the wet air masses of the Atlantic and Pacific oceans. But the northern third of the vast African continent was dominated by the Sahara, possibly the largest and driest of the world's great deserts. The Mediterranean, the Roman's "sea between the land," therefore separated two radically different climatic zones.

Unlike the Caribbean, which channels the thermal energy and moisture of the tropics up the Mississippi Basin and into the heartland of North America, the Med was insulated from the tropics by the expanse of the Sahara. Accordingly, sailors in America were used to a much different pattern of weather than that found in the Med and were often unprepared for the violence of the storms here.

I well remembered the reaction of some navy aviators off the *J. F. Kennedy* who chartered our sloop *Piraya* in the early seventies. We got smacked by a late spring sirocco that blew up during the five hours of our return trip from Lindos to Rhodes. By the time we rounded the old limestone fort of Saint Nicholas tower and dropped our double-reefed mainsail in Mandraki harbor, even these seasoned Phantom pilots were thoroughly impressed by the sudden, savage turn in the weather. Earlier that day, they had stretched out on the foredeck to absorb the benevolent May sunshine and marvel at the ripe translucent blue of the Aegean. Three hours later, they were hanging on grimly in the cockpit while the boat staggered and plunged through a dirty southeast swell, beneath a low overcast that slashed past above us at 40 knots.

One of the pilots, a mustachioed lieutenant commander with a Vietnam tour behind him, was especially impressed. "Where the *hell* did this weather come from?" he asked, shaking the spray from his dripping face. "I never saw a storm develop so fast."

At the time, I knew more about sailing than I did about Mediterranean weather and had been just as shocked as him by the sudden arrival of a force eight blow. But over the next few years, I made a point of learning about the region's weather systems. One of the first things I came to recognize was how much further north the Med was than the Caribbean and the Gulf of Mexico. In fact, the southernmost spot in the Med was at a higher latitude than the northern shore of the gulf. Also, the eastern Med was bounded by the arid bulk of Arabia and Southwest Asia, not by the ocean. The deserts of North Africa and the Middle East cannot feed moist, unstable air into the temperate zones of the north. Europe and the Soviet Union, therefore, rarely experience the same violent atmospheric collisions that spawn hundred-mile squall lines and clusters of tornadoes across North America every spring and summer when hot, wet gulf air strikes Canadian cold fronts.

Also, the high European latitudes—relative to North America—

result in a different flow of jet streams, those fast stratospheric rivers that weave invisibly above us to dominate our daily weather. During the six winter months when the sun is below the equator, the European jet streams tend to dip south toward the Med. Often the flow will kink or wobble, and a weak upper-level low will suddenly deepen into a closed-surface depression with a very steep barometric gradient.

On the newspaper weather maps, these lows often appear over the Iberian Peninsula, sometimes straddling the Pyrenees. As the depression moves east, the land forms of the Alps and Balkans influence the size and shape of the trough. Occasionally, a deep, energetic maritime low from the Atlantic will sweep in to skirt the northern littoral of the Med and deepen further, stalled against a high-pressure ridge dominating Soviet Asia. When this occurs, surface winds across most of the Mediterranean shift to the south-southeast in accordance with the low's cyclonic, counter-clockwise flow. Because these depressions can form or deepen so rapidly, with little warning, the wind effect in the Med is difficult to forecast.

Like many jaded expat sailors in Greece, I used to blame the wildly inaccurate maritime weather forecasts on the general incompetence of Greek technicians. Then, one summer when I was visiting navy friends aboard an American missile frigate in Piraeus, I learned from the ship's meteorological officer just how unpredictable weather was in this part of the world.

He brought up the notorious case of the USS *Bache*, a Sixth Fleet destroyer that had anchored off Rhodes harbor in the winter of 1968, the first liberty call the crew had enjoyed during a protracted deployment following the Six Day War the previous summer. Naturally enough, the captain allowed most of the crew ashore to sample the pleasures of Rhodes's bountiful and cheap liquor and reputedly numerous Scandinavian tourist women. In the time between the noon liberty boat and sunset, a vicious sirocco blew up out of the cloudless sky, formed a dirty force ten line squall, and dragged the *Bache* all the way across the anchorage and onto the reef at the entrance to Mandraki harbor. Before the skeleton crew could get power up and maneuver, the *Bache* broke her back on the rocks. Only a valiant and skillful rescue operation by the Greek coast guard and local fishermen saved the watch on board from certain death in the high surf smashing the sea wall. The ship itself was unsalvageable.

After the court of inquiry, the weather officer told me, the disgraced captain probably was given command of a used-paint depot in North Dakota. But, my friend insisted, the tragedy had not been entirely the captain's fault. "The weather over here is a bastard," the officer muttered, shaking his head. "Anybody who tells you the Med's a lake is either stupid or ignorant . . . or both."

From that officer, and from other professional meteorologists I'd encountered over the years, I had learned more about the Med's *bastard* weather. The sudden violence of these southeast blows could be explained in part by the "slot" effect of the northern shore's topography. Mountain chains—the Pyrenees, the Massif Central, the Alps, and the Carpathian Mountains—are broken by a few relatively narrow river systems: the Rhône, the Danube, and the Volga valleys. These are the "slots" through which the southern winds must be channeled to fill the depressions moving north of the mountains. As any high-school physics student learns about the Venturi effect, when a fluid stream is compressed, its speed increases. Hence the sudden violence of siroccos, the generic term—of Genoese origin like so many Mediterranean nautical expressions—given to these autumn and spring storms.

But the slot effect of the mountains and valleys plays just as important a role in the formation and strength of the summer "etesian" wind systems that American sailors find just as disconcerting when they first cruise the Med. In the west, these cold, clear-air northerlies are called the mistral. The bora of the Adriatic is slightly less violent. But the Aegean meltemi, in my opinion, is the most unpredictable and vicious.

Every summer sailing season in Greece for the previous ten years, I'd met American or British yacht sailors who'd had their first encounter with the meltemi. Inevitably, their reaction had been shock, then a certain outrage that nature could be so underhanded as to throw full *gales* at them, day after day for a week at a time, from out of the cloudless, aching blue sky. The habitual clear weather and high, steady barometer of the summer Aegean has confused many skippers sailing the Greek islands for the first time. Where they come from, a gale is associated with a falling barometer, backing winds, and, above all, overcast skies. Unfortunately, etesian winds do not work that way.

The dynamics of these winds involve the formation of static clear-weather lows in the desert heartland of the Middle East—often centered over Jordan and Israel—and wide continental high-pressure ridges in eastern Europe. As these unequal atmospheric systems pulse and contract on roughly seven-day cycles each summer, masses of cool, dry air rush down the "slots" of the Danube and Volga valleys; this air flow is further constricted by the mountains of the Balkans and Anatolia and channeled across the Aegean, en route to the baking summer low in the Levant.

To exacerbate the meltemi's strength, the wind often bounds over steep, naked stone island ridges, producing savage down-drafts—invisible 60-knot tubes of wind that blast unsuspecting sailors who have sought *shelter* by sailing the ostensibly protected leeward passages along the eastern shores of these mountainous islands.

The word "meltemi" comes from the medieval Genoese expression for clear weather: *bel tempo*, but the term was never intended to mean *good* weather. In the Aegean, that expression is also transmuted Italian, *bonitsa*, and connotes the gentle westerly breezes of an Aegean high-pressure system. With a meltemi, however, the word *gentle* is not applicable. The wind has an uncompromising on-off quality to it. Typically, the meltemi blows from mid-June to late September and follows patterns that seem tantalizingly predictable but usually defy the weather forecasters.

Days on which the meltemi blows usually begin hot and clear, generally windless; the sea is the flat plum blue of the Aegean summer. Around 10:00 A.M., the sky seems to harden to a deep cobalt; evaporation haze disappears, and the wind begins with kitten paws from the west-northwest. An hour later, there's a definite northwest breeze rising. By three, the wind is chugging out of the northwest, raising that short, lumpy sea. As the afternoon wears on, there is 40 knots, howling down from the northwest, blasting over the mountainous islands. The channels of the Cycladese and Dodecanese are fields of white water, with wave crests offshore above fifteen feet and miserably close together, almost impossible conditions for those trying to beat their way north.

The meltemi, like most winds, will usually abate with sunset. But, during typical three-day blows that occur throughout the season, the wind will rise again after dark and blow with renewed intensity all night, finally dropping just before dawn. The next day, the wind will mount again several hours earlier than it did the first day. Some years this pattern can repeat itself day after day for weeks. In 1971, Carol and I suffered through eighteen straight days of meltemi when we ran *Piraya* as a charter boat.

Most experienced charter skippers in the Aegean plan careful strategies to outwit the meltemi. They often make their northerly progress in the early predawn hours, motor-sailing into the narrow channels when the wind is either flat or at its weakest. By midday, if the meltemi is up, they reach east or west to take the wind on the beam and spare their charter guests the wet, pounding discomfort of a beat into the unrelenting wind and pyramid seas.

In the mid-1970s, I met a young American captain named Phil who had just completed his first full year sailing his sixty-foot steel ketch in Greece, a year that had been marked by especially severe meltemis and terrible winter siroccos. "This goddamn place'll *kill* you, if you give it half a chance," he complained one night over a tin carafe of retsina at Manolis's fish café in Rhodes's Old Town. "All summer long the meltemi hammers you from the northwest. Then, as soon as the rainy season starts, the siroccos clobber you from the southeast. Why the hell does anybody want to sail around here?"

I swigged some tarry retsina and snared a chunk of feta cheese from the communal salad bowl. "You heading back to the States, then?" I asked.

"Nah," he muttered. "I've invested too much time learning how to sail the Med to quit now. Besides," he added with a grin, "it *is* kinda pretty around here."

I poured him some more retsina and surveyed the other yacht sailors grouped around the rough wooden tables in the smoky, garishly lit café. Outside, a moaning sirocco blew above the orange tile roofs of the medieval city. Our boats were well secured inside Mandraki harbor; none of us had to face the sea tonight. We could speak magnaminously. At our table, Bill Sunday, a huge New Zealander foredeck man off *Stormvögel*, summed up what we all felt. "Hell, chum, look at it this way. If you can sail here, you can sodding well sail anywhere, can't you?"

Doug finished his soup first and volunteered to clean up the galley. Gratefully, Carol and I accepted his gesture. While he was below, I reset the wind vane, letting the bow fall off another twenty degrees to the northeast. Now we rode better, the motion eased, and we gained at least a knot. To the west, overcast was rapidly filling the sky. A wide cirrus plume spread directly overhead, blending into dirty cirro-stratus. Carol looked tired and apprehensive as she crouched opposite me in the windy cockpit. I scowled at the swell and the sky.

"Let's fall off some more," I suggested. "We can make our landfall further up the coast. That way, we'll get some lee from the island."

She sat up and studied the sea, then squinted back aft at the building depression's sky signs. "If this isn't a real sirocco," she said slowly, reasoning it out, "then we'll lose twenty or thirty miles by reaching up the coast of Sardinia."

Again, I stared at the mounting swell. "But if it is a real blow, we'll lose that much tacking back and forth on the rhumb line."

She silently nodded.

I bent to free the vane's tiller lines. "Besides," I said, trying to sound cheerful, "it'll be fun to reach with this wind. Isn't this trip *supposed* to be fun once in a while?"

Carol rose to ease the mainsheet. She was smiling now. "That's what the travel agent said when she sold us this cruise."

With the sails eased and the swell on the starboard beam, *Matata* rose to meet each wave. She stroked through the troughs and slid up the swell faces. Ahead of us, the high gray stratus leached out the blue dome of sky. We sat easily in the cockpit now, eating blood-red Spanish grapes, absorbed by the graceful strength of our boat.

I SAT UP with Malcolm in the damp, windy night when he relieved my watch. As sometimes happened, I was reluctant to go to sleep after a dark and lonely two hours in the cockpit. I wanted to talk, or at least to sit close to him for a little while. Several times crossing the Atlantic I had experienced a kind of vertigo, as if the boat were going downhill in the black night, a very eerie feeling. This happened especially on moonless nights when there was not enough starlight to give the horizon definition and one lost all points of reference. Tonight I had felt this vertigo again and had had a hard time overcoming the associated anxiety.

I made coffee, then joined Mal above. He was busy resetting the wind vane, refining the usual five-degree meander along our rhumb line down to a tad less. It was very dark in the cockpit, the only light coming from a slight reflection off the water of our stern light and the dull yellow compass lamp. As Mal pulled in the Walker log line to take out a kink, I heard him give a muted shriek. Automatically, I reached out to grab him, my hand clenching around his ankle as he leaned over the stern.

"It's okay, just look." I couldn't see a thing. Mal struggled over the tiller lines to shelter with me in the lee of the cabin. He had something in his hands.

A small land bird, a beige and red finch, had landed on our deck. It was soaking wet and cool, but alive. Its eyes stared weakly at us, but without fear; its head drooped with exhaustion. Mal and I looked at each other helplessly. What could we do for the tiny creature who had lost its way in this blow?

During the next half-hour we coaxed the bird to take some gruel made of crackers and milk. It seemed to revive and gave a little hop once or twice. The warmth of our cupped hands dried its feathers and, although it still shivered from time to time, its black eyes seemed more alert. Suddenly the little creature fluttered from my lap into the starboard cockpit well where we kept the sail ties and a winch handle. After turning several circles, the bird nestled down and fearlessly went to sleep.

On my next watch, the first thing I did was to peek into the well. The finch was still there. But late that afternoon, when we were expecting to pick up some indication of land, the bird poked its head out, stood on the cockpit cushion for a moment, nodded a few times, and took off. It flew straight to the northwest, as if it knew where it was going.

As we had feared, the wind dropped as we approached the hulking shadow of Sardinia. We had high green mountains in sight, although we couldn't make out the coastline yet, when I saw a small smudge to port. With Malcolm's 0900 sun sight and this landmark—the only small island anywhere near our course— we figured we were coming in a little north of our intended landfall. Until we were close enough to pick up some distinguishing features on Sardinia itself—such as lighthouse towers or distinctive capes—we would hold our course. When Malcolm came up for his watch at 1100 we sorted out the possibilities.

"I'd vote for a quiet night at anchor in that big bay, Golfo di Oristano, I think it's called," I said. "It should be right ahead of us. . . . Doesn't look like there's any town on the whole bay, but the chart marks several anchorages."

Malcolm looked at me closely, then faced ahead, toward the island. "Yeah, well . . . are you awfully tired?"

I knew what he was getting set to ask. Would I mind if we just kept sailing? We'd had a couple days of rough seas, but it had been calm for the past few hours and we'd managed to get some sleep. Doug was below deck now, determinedly taking a long morning lie-in.

"I guess we can just keep going," I said, trying not to let my disappointment show in my voice. Malcolm liked swinging at anchor in a quiet bay as much as I did. Although we were feeling a little rushed because we were behind our original schedule, we'd just been joking that we were supposed to be having fun, even if we were miserable—cold, wet, and seasick. So, I was surprised he didn't want to stop.

I guess I expected Malcolm to pick up on my disappointment anyway and say, "What the heck, let's go on in there and anchor for the night." But he didn't.

"The bay is shallow and open to the west," he began. Abruptly he turned to me. "Did you listen to the BBC last night?" he asked.

I peered at him. He looked tense, not exactly tired, but there were lines etched around the corners of his mouth. I hadn't bothered with getting the earphones out on my 0200 watch. Nor had I caught the early-morning broadcast we all usually listened to together over breakfast, preferring a little extra sleep.

Mal still wasn't looking right at me. "It seems . . . there's a report of an English girl who was abducted off a private yacht, here in Sardinia . . . a few days ago. And her kidnappers are asking for a huge ransom. They're like the local Mafia . . . the Ndragata they're called . . . "

"What?" I found it hard to believe. "That's crazy."

The story was repeated on the next news broadcast. The kidnappers were supposed to have taken this girl up into the mountains, somewhere in those shrouded, dark peaks right ahead of us, although the yacht itself and the rest of the crew were now safe in port. Obviously, anchoring for the night in a secluded bay was out. How would potential kidnappers know that we had hardly a *sou* to our name? No doubt, they thought anyone sailing around on a yacht must be rich.

The decision was clear; we had better stay out at sea.

I went below to study the chart. Soon, we picked up a landmark, the light tower on Capo della Frasca, and made our course change to 200 degrees magnetic, paralleling the coast southward. As I charted this new course, scanning for obstacles, marking the lights and capes en route and noting approximately the times we would see them, I saw that there was a small island just off the southwest corner of Sardinia. The chart showed a shipping channel marked with a myriad of lights and buoys. There seemed to be a lot of shoals and rocks, so we would be prudent to leave that island well to port.

I tapped the chart with my pencil. It would be foolish to attempt an unfamiliar channel like that at night, and it would be dead night when we got there. Or would it? I called up to Mal and Doug to take a bearing off the land again and see what kind of speed we were making. Since we were powering now with no wind, we might just make it to the entrance, have enough light to pick up the markers. . . . But that was stupid. We had definitely decided *not* to attempt any more of these adventurous nighttime approaches to confined waters. Then, looking closer, I saw that there was a little town marked on the small island, with a deep, protected harbor. Now Malcolm joined me at the chart table and we plotted the new bearings. I pointed at the town of Carlo Forte. "What do you think? Should we try it?"

He studied the chart, taking in my estimates of time. "Pretty close with dusk . . . "

"We might have the new moon before it's completely dark if these clouds clear just a little . . . and the channel looks well marked." For another five minutes we stared at the chart, measuring distances, Malcolm leaning over my shoulder. "I know we said we shouldn't risk these night approaches, but . . . "

"I know." Mal squeezed my shoulder and I knew we were going to do it. "This is what it's all about," he said. "We're experienced sailors and we know what we're doing. And I could really use some sleep tonight."

"Right. I'll work out the lights. Crank her up another knot."

He was already swinging up on deck. I could hear him nonchalantly telling Doug we were going into this little town that looked like a really safe anchorage. I smiled when he joked about not wanting to pass Italy without stopping for a pizza. With a light touch, he revved up the Volvo and we put on a bit more speed. After I had worked out a plan of attack on the channel, I handed up a list of the landmarks to check off, with the times I had estimated we would raise them. A few drops of rain fell on the card and smudged the notations.

"Time for oilskins again," Mal said, taking the card.

I passed them up and scanned the sky, hoping this was only a little shower, because we wanted some moon tonight. "You guys," I called above the sound of the engine, "I'm going to get an hour's shuteye. You're in charge." I knew I had to be well rested for the evening's adventure.

As I dozed off I realized that the excitement I was feeling was akin to what any sportsman feels in anticipation of competition. Only here, the competitors were the sea, the currents, the lights and buoys—which might, as we well knew, not be where they were supposed to be—and, of course, ourselves. There was risk and danger, but this crew and this boat were as well prepared as we could be. The alternative, "safe" course, of rounding the whole bottom of Sardinia and her satellite islands, presented no challenge.

CHAPTER SIX

OCTOBER 5
SARDINIA

R ain drifted in a fine, soaking veil, almost hiding the green slopes of Sardinia off to port. We powered south through a somber afternoon, the low overcast masking the nearby ridge-tops. Far out to sea, the sun was hidden as it slid beneath the cloud banks. I stood stiffly at the tiller, letting the rain bead on my stubbly beard. Soon it would be completely dark, and we would have to face yet another night approach to a strange harbor.

Our decision to avoid the exposed and shallow anchorage of the Golfo di Oristano had, no doubt, been correct. But I now felt a definite reluctance building inside me to seek shelter in the narrow shoal waters that lay five miles south of us. According to our Mediterranean Pilot, Carlo Forte, the port of the small satellite island of San Pietro, had a deep anchorage and offered the all-around protection of a concrete sea wall. We needed a rest after three uncomfortable nights at sea, and the only way any of us was going to have a full night's sleep was to make port. The alternative was to steer west out to sea for eight hours, then tack south for the balance of the night and try to pick up the light at Il Toro rock before dawn. With this unsettled weather, however, a night offshore promised to be anything but restful.

But the problems of threading our way into Carlo Forte seemed to worsen as the rainy daylight thickened around us into darkness. The channel between Isola San Pietro and the southwest coast of Sardinia proper was only two miles wide at its northern entrance. This channel was further constricted by shoals that swept out from both shores. On our American Navy chart, the approach to Carlo Forte harbor lay along a narrow two-fathom lane, marked by a series of light towers, flashing buoys, and unlit cans. To further confuse me, the navigational aids led to two harbors, Carlo Forte on the satellite island and Portoscuso, the petrochemical depot, on the "mainland" of Sardinia. As we motor-sailed down through the wet twilight, we would have to locate the proper entrance lane among the six alternating red and white sectors produced by the two light towers at the Secca Grande channel entrance.

I knew enough Italian to recall that *secca* meant "dry"; obviously that indicated shoal water. Once we were down in those shallows, we'd have to drop the main and crawl along at two knots, tiptoeing from buoy to buoy until we got a clear shot into Carlo Forte. If we had been here before in daylight, I wouldn't have been so anxious. But I hated the thought of repeating the light-that-wasn't-there fiasco of our approach on Ibiza.

I was preoccupied with these worries when Carol came up to the cockpit, dressed in a full suit of oilskins and boots, gingerly balancing two steaming mugs of tea. After handing me my tea, and wedging her own mug securely in a recessed scupper well, she dug into her jacket pocket. Inside a clear plastic baggie, she had secured a three-by-five card and one of the chart table penlights with a red bulb.

"I've got all the light and buoy sequences and the compass courses connecting them written down," she called above the rumble of the engine. "Once we make that light tower at . . . " she squinted down through the dripping baggie at her card, "ah, Isola Piana, we turn to a heading of 165 degrees magnetic and hold that for eight-tenths of a mile to a black-and-white can buoy. Then . . . "

With patient precision, Carol continued to recite all the steps of our safe approach to Carlo Forte. I smiled at her in sincere admiration. She'd even worked out the cross-bearings, so that we could verify our position as we crept down the dark channel. An Annapolis midshipman taking his final exam in coastal piloting could not have done better. What was so remarkable, I realized, was that piloting had not always been one of her particular seamanship skills. But in the past month, since we'd made our first European landfall at Cape Saint Vincent in Portugal, Carol had quietly taken it on herself to become the coastal pilot of this crew. She was the person who studied the List of Lights, detailed harbor plans, and the Mediterranean Pilot well in advance of each approach, so that we would not blunder into rocks or shoals on these night approaches. It was her meticulous piloting that brought us into Ibiza, despite the confusion with the lights.

I recognized now that it was her innate thoroughness and her organizational skills that made her such a natural pilot. She relished the precision, the advance planning needed to solve the riddles of a strange channel, just as I had come to love the delicate abstraction of celestial navigation out on the offshore reaches. We had been sailing together for ten years, and over that period we'd unconsciously worked out a pattern that divided the labors of seamanship quite equally between us.

But, in the beginning of our sailing careers, we'd both experienced a considerable transfer of the traditional gender chauvinism that then permeated our lives ashore. I had just resigned my Foreign Service position, a traditional enough job, despite its occasionally exotic venue. During most of my years with the government, I'd put on a shirt and tie each morning and driven off to an office, while Carol had tried with varying success to balance the demands of a hectic diplomatic social life with her work as an editor and office manager. For the first six months in Greece, this pattern had continued, with my "office" being the whitewashed medieval tower of our Lindos house.

Once we took over *Piraya* as a charter sailboat, however, we were both thrown into an alien new environment where the old male-female roles did not always apply. Slowly, over the ensuing years, we developed informal patterns in which we learned to share the responsibilities of running a boat as a business. Often these patterns followed predictable routes; I became more proficient at engine repair and maintenance than Carol, and she was more skilled at cooking and provisioning. But neither of us felt the restrictive taboos that so many European and American couples seem to bring with them when they climb aboard a sailboat. Carol was just as capable as me when it came time to reef or change down sails; she could use the sextant and the radio direction finder, and she certainly was the better-skilled crew member when it came to taking and plotting bearings. Equally, I was a fanatic about tidiness and stowing below deck and general spit-and-polish throughout the boat. I was forever scrubbing the galley sinks and cleaning the head.

After a couple years in Greece, our sailing began to reflect the relaxed partnership, the noncompetitive cooperation that we nurtured in our new careers as free-lance writers. We were in this business together; we needed each other, and the old-fashioned ideas about what work was proper for a man or a woman simply did not apply to our lives. Most importantly, like many other couples running a business partnership, we developed a process of mutual decision making. Neither tried to dominate the other when we established priorities and set goals. Now, ten years into the experiment, I couldn't help but speculate on the effect sailing had had in the evolution of our human partnership.

Certainly, a boat was a microcosm, a compressed environment in which the tensions and joys of a couple's life were intensified. That, unfortunately, was probably why so many couples seemed to separate or quit sailing altogether after buying their dream boat and suffering their first disastrous offshore cruise. As an example of the inherent disharmony that afflicts many sailing couples, I'd noticed in the sailing magazines advertisements for T-shirts that proclaimed in bold print, "Don't shout at me!" A woman always appeared to be the model in the ads. Certainly, we'd encountered unexpected resentment and animosity in each other as we overcame our fears and learned to cruise safely offshore. But we had rarely become so frustrated that we considered giving up the sea. Now, for both of us, boats were no longer just a hobby; we'd reached that point where we unconsciously defined ourselves as sailors. Sailing now formed a large part of our identity. In many ways, cruising the planet's vast oceans in this small boat constituted who we were as people.

"There's going to be a problem with that oil refinery, or whatever all those colored lights are," Carol was saying.

I clicked my mind back from my speculations to focus on the problem at hand. The darkness was now complete, and a few miles to the southeast, dazzling yellow, red, and orange lights clustered around the petrochemical depot at Portoscuso. Some of these lights hung low along the black shore, others marched up the mountainside. Unfortunately, from our approach angle the flashing buoys marking our route across the shoals were lost against this confusing backdrop.

Carol called Doug up, and he took his station, facing forward on the starboard cockpit bench. His eyes were better than ours, and we were going to need his visual acuity to locate the unlit can buoys. Carol stood behind me on the vibrating lazaret, gripping the backstays with one hand to steady herself as she consulted her carefully organized approach card. We were in shoal water now. The rain seemed to coalesce into dark curtains as the overcast hunkered lower. The black-on-black silhouettes of the island ridges were eaten by the night, and I experienced a momentary swoop of disorientation, as if the boat were being irresistibly pulled to port.

The night before, twenty miles west of Capo San Marco, we had encountered strange rotating white marker beacons. When we'd first seen them, I'd been convinced that they were the distant San Marco lighthouse; then two more appeared to starboard, and, in a near panic, I'd steered almost due north for an hour, until I realized the lights were obstacle beacons floating low on the water, not lighthouses guarding the entrance to the Golfo di Oristano. The lights had probably been net markers of tuna trawlers, but they had quickly disorientated me, a good indication that the nautical equivalent of vertigo haunted all unfamiliar night approaches.

Carol bent to shine her red penlight on the face of the Walker taffrail log, our only reliable instrument since our depth sounder had packed up in the Azores six weeks ago.

"We should be getting that black-and-white buoy in about two minutes, Doug," she called, her voice level, seemingly unworried.

Doug rose on his knees and stared forward into the wet darkness. "Nothing yet."

I sat as calmly as I could, gazing into the faint orange glow of the compass as I held the tiller evenly in my sweating fingers. Once we made that buoy, we'd get some kind of idea what currents were at work in this shallow channel. The engine rumbled, the rain whispered down through the darkness. Carol and Doug stared ahead, searching for the unlit buoy.

Two minutes went by. Five minutes, then eight. "I think we'd better . . . " I began.

"Buoy dead ahead!" Doug sang out. "Come port a little to miss her."

"Course change," Carol announced, as the dark metal can slid by the starboard beam. "Bring it down to one eight zero."

"One eight zero on the compass," I intoned. "What's the log read?"

"I've already logged it," Carol answered. "Four five seven point six. We'll get that red flasher in exactly one mile."

On this angle, the confused array of oil refinery lights was less of a factor in our piloting. We had made it through the most dangerous stretch. Suddenly, the palpable threat, the danger had vanished in the darkness. I found myself actually enjoying the challenge of this approach, relishing our competency, as we powered across the limestone bottom, only six feet beneath our keel.

"I think we can go back to cruising speed," I said, already reaching for the throttle.

"Let's wait till we get a bearing on that flasher," Carol answered, reaching down to touch the dripping shoulder of my jacket.

She was right, of course. Twenty more minutes out in the rain wouldn't get us any wetter than we already were. But, if there was unseen current in this channel, and we drifted across one of the *seccas* just east of our track and went aground at 6 knots, we could end up in real trouble. As was usually the case, her native caution was well balanced with my instinctive risk taking.

Ten minutes later, Doug called out the next light, and we had our clear channel in sight. Now the house lights of Carlo Forte began to crawl over the dark ridge that sheltered the town north of the harbor. In the binoculars, I could see that the village was whitewashed stone, with the usual tile roofs of the Mediterranean. Tall, well-tended palm trees stood out in the street lamps strung along the low esplanade. As we powered slowly toward the flashing green and red lamps at the harbor entrance, we could see just how attractive a town Carlo Forte was. It had all the elements one associates with a postcard Mediterranean port—colorfully painted fishing boats at anchor, a palm-lined corniche, shady squares, and a gracefully spired church. There was almost no vehicle traffic and only a few strollers on the wide field-stone sidewalks along the quay.

We chugged slowly into the inner harbor, and suddenly I realized that there were no other yachts moored along the quay. Certainly, there were no lime-green laser beams proclaiming the latest trendy disco to the gangs of jaded young tourists. From what I could see, there did not appear to be any tourists at all, young or old, jaded or enraptured.

Swinging away from the quay, we drifted free and went to work placing fenders and dock lines. As I secured the bow line, I happened to look across the dark channel that separated us from the industrial complex of Portoscuso. In the wet night, the refinery and petro-chemical plant looked like a distant volcano, trembling orange flames and dense, billowing smoke. From Carlo Forte harbor, we had a clear view of the cracking towers and gas flares of the complex, a scene that had been blocked on our earlier approach. What we now saw could properly be described with that shop-worn Victorian adjective "Sty-gian": dark mounds of noxious steam, bottom lit with rippling fire-balls, the entire complex seemingly dominated by primordial forces left over from an earlier geological epoch.

The rainy breeze rose for a moment, then dropped, bringing with it a definite industrial stench, bad eggs and scorched copper, a *petite madeleine* messenger from the sophomore chemistry lab at the University of Wisconsin. Beneath the cloying overcast, the plant's fumes spread across the channel to taint the atmosphere of this pretty little port. The smog wasn't strong enough to make our eyes smart, but there was no denying the presence of industrial pollution.

Doug looked up from securing a fender at the starboard beam. "Is the oil refinery making that smell?" he muttered.

"Yep." I nodded. "They call that *progress.*"

Doug shook his head. "Smells like the whole town had beans for lunch."

Carol was at the helm. "I'm sure the locals get used to it after a while." She smiled wanly. "Especially on pay-day. Sardinia *is* a very poor island, you know."

I swung aft to coil the last dockline. She was right, of course; all over the Mediterranean people in picturesque villages like Carlo Forte have had to swallow the caustic discharges and smoke of heavy industry. Traveling in Spain, Italy, Yugoslavia, and Greece, we'd seen that rapid industrial growth completely outpaced environmental planning in the quarter-century between the Marshall Plan and the OPEC oil embargo of the mid-1970s. Much of this expansion occurred in impoverished backwaters like Sardinia, Calabria, and Sicily. In Greece, petrochemical and cement plants sprang up on the Peloponnesos around the artificial harbors that offered easy access to cargo vessels. Our Italian friends told us that they didn't even have a word in their own language to describe the economic explosion. *Il Boom*, they called it.

And, sadly, during the heyday of prosperity that inevitably accompanied the new industrial growth, people tended to ignore the warnings of the environmentalists. Many of the regions benefiting most from the post-war economic miracle had been chronically poor. A newly built plastics factory or a foundry in Calabria might poison the marine environment for ten kilometers up and down the coast, but the industry brought unprecedented wealth to villages that had lived at the subsistence level for centuries. If the local mackerel shoals disappeared when the coastal water acquired the bilious yellow of the cement plant's effluent, villagers could afford to buy their mackerel in cans, the product of Korean factory ships half a world away. A person could forget about the Agip refinery's noxious presence if he could now afford a Sony color television and spend his evenings watching Juventis of Rome trounce the hated Munich soccer team for the European Cup.

But, by the late 1970s, the governments of the Mediterranean countries could no longer close their eyes to the unmistakable environmental tragedy around them. The Mediterranean Sea was sick; some said it was critically ill, that it had already passed a tip point and was facing biological extinction. The familiar catalogue of villains was exhibited: accumulated agricultural pesticides, industrial poisons like PCBs, PBBs, and the various deadly sulfides of lead and mercury, unchecked rivers of raw sewage, acid rain, oil spills, and, of course, overfishing. Then, in a series of international conferences that saw traditional enemies like Greece and Turkey, Syria and Israel temporarily bury their animosities, difficult and sweeping political decisions were reached.

Basically, the countries agreed to finally stop using the Mediterranean Sea as a bottomless sewer and toxic waste dump. All future industrial development on the Mediterranean coastline would have to meet minimum environmental standards. Existing plants would be modified to curb the worst discharge abuses, and the dumping of untreated sewage would, in theory at least, be completely abolished by the mid-1980s. The governments also addressed the chronic problems of overfishing and again established minimum regional standards on net sizes, methods, and species quotas that would allow the marine food chain to regenerate. Citing hard statistics that linked oil spills with declining tourism, the governments unanimously agreed to enforce more strictly the existing regulations governing tanker operations in their territorial waters.

As these environmental conferences evolved, cynics complained that the proposed reforms were so much whitewash, given the voracious corporate greed and governmental corruption and inefficiency prevalent in the Med. But, slowly, even the most cynical observers came to agree that the countries sharing the Mediterranean coastline seem to be sincere in their collective will to save their common sea.

When the Greeks—whom many considered among the worst offenders—actually jailed a *Greek* tanker captain for pumping his bilges and leaving a wide tar deposit on the beaches of Crete, environmentalists began to recognize that the Med might be rescued from extinction after all.

As we putted through the sleeping harbor of Carlo Forte, however, there was no way to escape the chemical stench of the industrial complex across the channel. No doubt the emissions were within current guidelines. Probably the plant's discharges were carefully monitored and every effort was taken to avoid toxic spills. For all I knew, the refinery might be considered a model site, a goal to which its Turkish and Moroccan counterparts might one day aspire. But the rotten-egg flatus of the gas flares and cracking towers remained, a tangible reminder that we lived in a time of unpleasant compromise. There was no such thing, I realized, as a completely clean industry. It might not have been fashionable to admit this, but I felt many environmentalists who demanded unrealistic standards were shrill hypocrites when it came to condemning the greedy, polluting corporations. Usually these critics considered the cornucopia of the industrial twentieth century—cheap, abundant energy, private automobiles, multi-use polyesters, convenient air transport, and, of course, bountiful and inexpensive food—to be a basic perquisite due every member of modern society.

Many of us wanted the goodies, the comfort of polyester, the ease of Teflon, but we sure as hell wouldn't admit that those chemicals were synthesized in the stinking tanks and flaming towers of plants like that one across the channel. We demanded kiwi fruit and navel oranges in our supermarkets, then railed against the semi-trucks crowding the highways. We muttered bitterly about acid rain killing our beautiful forests, then went up to watch "Great Performances" on the color TV in our bedroom, while the lights in the den burned uselessly all night.

It was certainly sad when the lovely, wild coast of Sardinia was blighted with an oil refinery, but we all used oil, we all wanted the freedom of a private car, the convenience of gas heating and cooking. The people of the Med were like the rest of us. And, in the headlong stampede for wealth and comfort that followed the protracted and bloody devastation of World War II, they had almost murdered their sea; certainly, they had critically wounded its ecosystem. It would be decades before the Mediterranean was healthy again, and certain districts—perhaps this corner of Sardinia—might never recover. But I would be among the worst of the hypocrites if I stood in the cockpit of this sleek epoxy-resin sailboat and cursed the voracious capitalists who had built the stinking industrial cauldron that bubbled and flared out there in the rainy Mediterranean darkness.

CARLO FORTE

When Mal and Doug finished tying the spring lines on the stone quay, I was amazed to discover it was only 9:00 P.M. The difficult approach to Carlo Forte through the channel had seemed to take much longer than two hours. Around us, the quiet town also made me think it was closer to midnight.

"What about dinner ashore?" I suggested, handing the men mugs of coffee as they came back on board.

"I guess so," Mal said looking at the dead town. "But I suppose we should check into Italy or something." There was no official-looking person anywhere in sight, however.

Across the wide quay—actually an extension of the town's waterfront piazza—was a blockish, three-floor hotel. A light inside the high entranceway cast a warm long oblong in our direction. There would be a restaurant inside. "I think we could just go across there," I said, pointing at the hotel, "and no one would care. We can do the customs in the morning."

An old waiter in a threadbare white jacket ushered us into the chilly dining room. After smiling politely through our rusty Italian, he assured us that he understood our order. Then he led us to a central table heaped with a cold antipasto buffet and disappeared through the swinging door to the kitchen. The second course consisted of delicate stuffed tortellini in a clear broth. Obviously, we were being served the house menu, but it was so good I wasn't about to argue. To cap the best meal we'd had since leaving the Azores, our waiter next brought us fine, young veal scaloppini in a light cream sauce. The carafe of local white wine accompanying this epicurean repast was strong and a little tarry, but it blended well. After fruit cups and coffee, the old man presented the bill, less than fifteen dollars in lire. I handed Malcolm the thin booklet of American Express traveler's checks.

"Oh, no, we can't take those," the waiter said emphatically.

The bank wouldn't be open until Monday, and this was Friday night. We certainly didn't want to get stuck here for two whole days just to change a little money. Malcolm tried to explain while I searched my purse for the dollar singles I had tucked away.

The waiter waved away my fistful of green money. "Tomorrow is good," he said in accented English. "*Señora patrona* here tomorrow."

Well, it was an island and we were on a boat and could easily leave without paying our bill, but obviously strangers were trusted here. This easygoing manner was a welcome change from the suspicion and antipathy we had experienced in Ibiza and Almeria.

In the morning, a small fishing fleet of green and yellow dories came into the harbor and began docking around us. One of the skippers indicated the sea wall extending from the other end of the piazza. After some discussion, we realized that yachts were supposed to moor over there, that this was a "working" quay. Once we were secured on the other side of the harbor, a sleepy-looking customs official wandered over and led Malcolm to his office to issue our *manifèsto*. Meanwhile, Doug and I attached the hose to a water point and, wildly shivered in the cold morning air, rinsed the salt accumulation off the boat and ourselves.

When Malcolm returned with our stamped passports we each took off in a different direction on necessary errands. I, as usual, went in search of fresh provisions. As I crossed the shady piazza, I could feel I was being watched. In the shadow of tall palm trees, on benches scattered among the trimmed ornamental shrubs and small oval flowerbeds, groups of men sat dozing. My passing appeared to be the highlight of their day, if not the week.

After I stocked my two canvas bags with tomatoes and zucchini at the open-air produce market behind the square, I visited the few shops. The last one along the street was a fresh pasta "factory." Inside, strands of linguine hung from drying racks and vast trays on the counter displayed an enormous variety of capellini, tortellini, penne, and other less familiar shapes of basic pasta. In my shaky Italian I pointed at what I wanted and chatted with a man in a floury white apron.

"You must be staying with Señora MacGregor," he insisted.

At first I couldn't understand what he was talking about. But soon I realized that the only other foreigners who regularly visited this village were an English family who had a house high up above the town. He had assumed that I, an English speaker, must somehow be related to them.

Strolling back toward the dock with my two full bags of purchases balancing me, I mused on how unspoiled Carlo Forte was. There was a slow, graceful charm about the people that showed that their old-fashioned country manners had not been touched by the prosperity that the petrochemical plant across the channel had brought. One fact I had learned from the *señora patrona*—who changed my traveler's check at a low rate of exchange, but at least she changed it—was that there was a regular ferry across to the "mainland." "Our sons, all the young people, go work there," she had said, gesturing widely toward Sardinia. That accounted too for the scarcity of pedestrians on the streets, and especially for the absence of young people.

I met Doug as I crossed the waterfront piazza. He had been equally impressed by the town and people. "Now this is what a Mediterranean island village should be like," I explained, "not all those weirdos in Ibiza."

We spotted Malcolm across the square, sitting on a bench eating a large chocolate ice cream cone. I joined him in the shade, and Doug went to the small shop on the corner and got us a couple of cones too. That next half-hour spent sitting in the pretty park licking our ice cream was the highlight of our shore excursions to date. There was an elegant tranquillity to the waterfront piazza with its palm trees, bitter orange hedges, and the sunny harbor, sheltering one clean white sailboat.

Soon I went back to *Matata* to stow the fresh provisions. Doug had already carted a block of ice over and chopped it into manageable hunks. All I had to do was rearrange the ice chest. While I was doing this, I suddenly heard Mal and Doug talking loudly up on the dock, and then I recognized the distinctive sounds of another yacht coming alongside the quay.

They were French, eight young men and women in sweaters and knit caps, aboard a one-off nine-meter sloop of shiny aluminum. The group was on their way to Tunisia, where Jean-Luc, the smiling owner, intended to winter the boat. As he waited for his turn with the water hose, the voluble young Frenchman explained that he had asked a few *copains* to help him sail the boat down to Bizerte. After years of observing the French sailing bareboats in the Aegean, I knew that their definition of "a few friends" was far different from our own. It constantly amazed me that the French relished sailing with so many people jammed aboard small boats, and I've never understood how they managed to eat, sleep, or even move around in such crowded conditions.

I suppose we seemed like relative hermits in comparison. And I realized that Mediterranean people often did not have the same regard for privacy and simple elbow room that we northerners valued so much. I'd seen whole extended Spanish families camping with a single tent, lined up on cots like wounded soldiers in a field hospital. Often, French yachts we'd encountered in Aegean anchorages had looked like refugee boats, their decks crowded with the inevitable hosts of *copains*, the rigging strung with drying laundry. If anything, the Italians carried this gang-vacationing to extremes. In Lindos, it was not uncommon for twenty-five or thirty young Italians on the *ferragosto* holiday to share a house that normally slept eight.

Our French neighbors on the overloaded ark of the aluminum sloop were a friendly lot, however, and I felt no resentment that they had joined us in this tranquil port. Obviously, they were enjoying their autumn cruise. That afternoon, the quay was lively with the music of their guitars and sweet, lilting folk songs.

We sailed at sunset, after studying the chart carefully and plotting our course southeast, past the west coast of Sicily and on to Malta. We still had over a thousand miles ahead of us before reaching Lindos and could not afford the lazy pleasure of another night in harbor. If the weather turned on us, or if we encountered headwinds, we could always duck into one of several ports along the western coast of Sicily. But now we had to leave Carlo Forte, the lovely village that somehow had been shielded from the armies of package tourists that had swept across the Mediterranean.

CHAPTER SEVEN

OCTOBER 8, SUNSET
30 MILES NORTH OF SKERKI BANK

We had been sailing beautifully for more than twelve hours. All day, the wind held steady in the northeast at 15 knots. The sky was pastel blue and free of haze, the horizons sharp, the sea almost flat. Between watches, I had slept in the sun while Carol cooked a fancy rigatoni lunch and Doug practiced his navigation, producing a flawless noon fix and some good afternoon moonlines. After the glowering rain of Sardinia, it seemed as if we were leaving autumn behind us in the Western Med, now that we were entering the Strait of Sicily.

When the sun was low, and we'd had our usual crew conference around the chart to plan our night's sailing, Carol announced that she intended to give us yet another special meal, a ragoût of fresh veal and mushrooms, served with leeks and new potatoes steamed in the pressure cooker. To add to the festivities, I opened an iced bottle of the good Sardinian white wine we'd bought in Carlo Forte.

I was slightly apprehensive, however, about the shoal water that lay to the south and the Egadi islands that guarded our approach to Capo Boeo, the western extremity of Sicily. If the weather suddenly went bad on us and we got smacked by a sirocco similar to the levanter that had hit us approaching the Strait of Gibraltar, we'd have to tack north and south of our course. That would take us down to the banks off the north coast of Tunisia; Keith Reef lay down there, an unlighted rock only twenty-four miles below our rhumb line. I also knew that tacking all night in a short, crashing sea and unpredictable currents around those islands wouldn't be much fun. So I couldn't entirely relax when we brought the wine up to the cockpit and toasted the lavender sunset and the bright evening star rising on the port bow.

But the barometer was rock steady, and there hadn't been any telltale cirrus or frozen jet contrails in the western sky to indicate an approaching depression. Indeed, this sky was as benevolent as any we'd seen out on the blue longitudes of the Azores High. Down at the chart table, Carol had opened the wide British Admiralty Eastern Mediterranean Sea sheet. She gripped the bronze dividers and walked off our intended track to Lindos: Sicily to Malta; Malta to Crete; Crete to Rhodes . . . 1,100 nautical miles. If this weather somehow held and we had easy reaches, we could log over 100 miles a day, just as we had in the Atlantic. Even with visits to Malta and Crete, we could be in Lindos in less than two weeks, ample time to enjoy the fine fall sailing weather that often seemed to linger around Rhodes a few weeks longer than in the rest of the Aegean.

As I had watched Carol marking our planned course with the dividers, I felt swelling within me a sense of confidence that the headwinds and depressions we'd experienced from Gibraltar to Sardinia were truly behind us. The Western Med was actually a branch of the Atlantic, I reasoned, dominated by the cruel weather of that ocean, but the *Eastern* Med, the southern lobe of this Middle Sea, was more benign, a sheltered lake that would give us an unbroken stretch of these easy days, force-four northerlies, cloudless skies, a gentle, lapping sea.

As I swung up to the foredeck to check the sails and rigging for chafe before dark, I smiled at my Pollyanna musings. The Eastern Med could, of course, kill you in a twinkling; as that frigate's weather officer had told me, only a fool would underestimate this sea. But ... I still couldn't shake my optimism. Luck did move in cycles; we'd already had our run of nasty weather. Maybe this high pressure would stall for a week or ten days, enough time for us to make good our long reach to the east. Why not?

I sat on the bow pulpit and tugged the thick forestay, my fingers jammed between the genoa luff and the stainless steel cable. The smooth white curve of the sail climbed above me to the masthead. In fifteen minutes, it would be time for navigation lights. Now, I could balance here, feeling the boat ride this breeze, hissing along at 5 knots through the calm water, perfectly balanced on its two sails, the wind vane steering without strain, smack on the southeast rhumb line for the western cape of Sicily. Carol and Doug were sitting on the highside of the cockpit, chatting over their plastic tumblers of wine. Down on the gimbaled stove the pressure cooker wheezed and chattered.

I sipped my own iced wine, savoring the moment. Had I owned a good camera and been a better photographer, I might have stood on the bow pulpit, steadying myself on the stay and focused aft, along the graceful shoulder of the deck and cabintop, heeled against the darkening twilight sea, toward the hard line of the western horizon that still held the plum and tangerine flares of the sunset. This was a picture for a sailing magazine: a peaceful evening in the Med, sailing at its finest, the crew, the boat, and the sea, all in balanced harmony.

"Hey," Doug called, rising from the port cockpit bench to point south. "Dolphins down there . . . big ones. Wow! Look how they're splashing . . . "

Carol was upright beside him now, staring toward the south, her face a mixture of happy curiosity and sudden, frowning worry. The white expanse of the genoa blocked my view to starboard, so I trotted aft, swinging instinctively along the shrouds and grab rails, guarding my wine glass against the chest of my sweatshirt.

"I don't think those were dolphins," Carol said with soft precision as I slid down into the cockpit. "They looked so *big,* and I never saw dolphins . . . *smack* the water that way."

I grabbed the binoculars and scanned the stretch of water at which she was pointing. Nothing, just blue-gray ripples, thickening to darkness with the twilight. After checking the compass course and the sail trim against the tension on the wind vane's tiller lines, I sat down on the cockpit bench. The plastic cushion was beaded with the first evening dew. In a minute, I'd need my light nylon deck pants. Soon it would be full night, and we'd eat our festive meal, then split into watches to sleep or take the helm.

Carol stared forward, steadying herself with one hand on the boom. "I'd better look at those potatoes," she said. "We can eat in . . ."

"Jesus *Christ!*" Doug yelled. He lurched over the starboard rail, then threw himself backward toward the companionway.

I was shocked at his outburst and guessed that he must have stubbed his bare toes, or cut his foot on something sharp. I half-rose to help him; then I saw the long black shape in the water, not six feet from the starboard quarter.

"Oh my God!" Carol whispered. "A *whale.*" Her hand went to her mouth in spontaneous reaction. Her eyes expanded, then she squinted in fear. "No . . . wait, there's *two* of them."

I found myself up on the lazaret, my left knee jammed painfully against a docking cleat, my right hand snagged up on the backstays to support my weight as I stared down. The smooth water of our quarter wave seemed to swell, to billow up with a glistening dark bubble. Another elongated cylinder of thick black water slid parallel to the first, and together, the two dark, liquid tubes flowed toward us, silently, with slow precision, as if pushed by unseen hydraulic pistons.

Hanging awkwardly against the lowside lifelines, my knees and ankles twisted, I was not immediately able to recognize what I saw. But, a moment later, the image registered. Two gray-black pilot whales, each over twenty feet long, were closing in on the boat, thrusting their solid, combined weight against the starboard waterline. Now I clearly recognized their bulbous heads, their taut, glistening skins, and their mammalian eyes.

A rush of adrenalin heated my limbs and torso. Those goddamned things were going to roll us over. For some bizarre reason, two supposedly harmless pilot whales had decided to gang up on us, to throw their bulk upward from beneath the exposed stern quarter. They were right *there*, jostling together, heaving against the waterline. Had I the courage, I could have patted the streaming bulges of their heads.

We all hung there, the three humans and the two whales, for a frozen moment of indeterminate length. Then the outward whale wheezed, blew a steamy breath from his blowhole, and slid onto his side, exposing a white oval patch beneath his jaws. His curving black pectoral fin flapped loudly against his partner's flank, sending a cloud of spray into the cockpit. Two broad tails stroked and splashed. I could feel *Matata* heave under me.

Without conscious decision, my survival senses took charge. "Start the engine," I yelled at Carol.

She dove through the companionway toward the main circuit breakers.

"Give me the air horn, quick!" I screamed at Doug.

He, too, reacted without hesitation.

In my mind, I had superimposed the images of the sleeping sperm whale we'd almost struck during our night approach on the Azores and the silent killer whales that had stalked past our bow in the foggy Strait of Gibraltar. My mouth was dry, my gut trembling. In a second, these two animals would porpoise up across the rail, to overpower our ballast with their mass. The boat would broach, sails and rigging in the water, the sea pouring through the open hatches. Twenty seconds later, *Matata* would sink, and we would find ourselves flailing about in the darkness, suffering through the last moments of panic before we died.

Doug banged the metal trumpet of the freon horn into my fist, and I grabbed for the instrument, fumbling in my panic, my gaze stuck to the glossy dark head of the nearest whale. Just as I hit the horn lever, the engine rumbled to life under me. I blasted the horn, twice, four times . . . eight, long, harsh rips of noise. The diesel engine roared now. I aimed the horn directly at the whales' dark snouts, where I knew their sensitive echo-ranging organs were found.

Their reaction was startling. Rearing back like angry cattle in a stockyard chute, they squeaked in protest. A black tail pounded the water; a white throat flashed, and curved fins clattered against the topsides of the boat. As they porpoised away in panic, the smaller, innermost whale rolled her oil-barrel head toward me and seemed to wince, the black flesh constricting around her soft, bovine eye. Then the pressure wave of their tail flukes hit us, and the boat rolled hard to port. I was thrown into the tangle of the wind vane tiller lines. I moaned in uncontrollable fear. All I could think of was those two enraged pilot whales, rounding on us out there in the darkness to come careening back, unseen below the surface. They would hit the boat in the flat bilge sections and send us hard over on the port rail. I would be caught in this spider web of lines when the boat went down.

Thrashing clumsily, I freed the tiller lines, thrust the gear lever forward, and threw the helm hard over. Doug snatched up the freon horn and continued blasting as I steered due north, opposite the course the panicked whales had chosen. Now I saw Carol halfway up the companionway, the black plastic flare pistol case in her right hand. "Grab some lifejackets," I yelled. Her face went chalky beneath her deep tan, but she didn't question my order. A moment later, she slung three orange lifejackets up to the cockpit, followed by the yellow tote bag of our emergency signal equipment.

The genoa backed hard against the starboard shrouds as we sped north, into the eye of the wind. But my attention was focused behind us, toward the dark water where the whales had sounded. Time flowed again, and I released the muscles of my chest and belly. Five minutes, and the whales had not shown themselves. I felt suddenly foolish seeing Carol and Doug with their bulging orange lifejackets laced up tight beneath their chins. In the remaining daylight, they appeared utterly tragic, wearing these unmistakable accoutrements of disaster. Lifejackets were objects I was used to handling when I opened the quarterberth to service the engine, but when I saw Carol actually wearing one, I felt a confused muddle of emotions. Had I overreacted? Were those whales simply curious, playful mammals, no more threatening than dolphins?

But then I let myself remember the heaving thrust of the whales' pressure wave, the weight of their flanks against the starboard quarter. Even if they had been playing with us, the combined mass of those two animals could have capsized the boat.

"How big would you say they were?" My voice was squeaky with vestigial adrenalin.

"Damn big," Doug muttered.

Carol frowned. "When the one closest was right against the boat, he stretched from the transom to the shrouds . . . " She stared at the starboard rigging. "How long is that?"

"Fifteen feet," I answered. "Maybe more."

As the darkness clotted into night, we stood down from our vigil in stages, none of us eager to discuss our feelings. First, Doug released the backed genny and sheeted it in on the starboard tack. Later, I slowed the engine to half-speed. Carol collected the lifejackets and stowed them below; Doug retrieved the spilt wine bottle from the cockpit well. Before she came back up, Carol lit the running lights.

"I turned off the stove when I started the engine," she said, staring into the darkness aft. "I can heat the food again . . . or, we can wait."

"I'm not real hungry," Doug replied.

"Let's wait a while," I added.

Twenty minutes later, we tacked over to our original heading and I killed the engine. It was full night now, well past eight o'clock. No moon, but distant bands of cold stars gave dimension to the sky. We were sailing well again, the vane set, the quarter wave hissing softly.

"I think they were trying to push against the boat so they could mate," Carol said, choosing her words slowly, reasoning the problem as she spoke. "They need something, some solid point for leverage. . . . They must have thought we were another whale."

"Lucky Pierre," Doug said, and we all laughed inordinately at his gamey humor.

I should have been able to relax, but the black distance toward the south held me. There was no way to fully reconstruct the splintered moments when the whales actually thrust against the boat, no way to validate my actions. If I had panicked, at least I'd erred on the side of caution. I could easily accept responsibility for what I'd done. But, despite Carol's reasoned explanation, I couldn't dispel the feeling that this gentle pastel sea had *turned* on us with sudden, irrational treachery. Pilot whales were simply great big dolphins; they weren't supposed to threaten boats, as that pair had menaced us. A calm sunset with all the elements of wind and weather finally working in our favor should not have unexpectedly degenerated into a matter of survival. If that were true, I realized, the sea was not the rational environment that I had grown to expect. If those two Marine Land pets, those smiling squeakers of the dolphin tank, could abruptly menace a boat like this and try to smash it, then the sea was, ultimately, a place that I would never understand.

That bleak speculation clung to me as we sailed east through the starry darkness.

NO ONE FELT like sleeping after the confrontation with the whales. I surely didn't want to get caught snuggled in my sleeping bag in the dark cabin if and when they should return to play push-and-shove with *Matata*. At midnight, therefore, all three of us were still in the cockpit, straining in the rising moonlight to find the lighthouse on Marettimo Island. That light would give us a reference for the course change to Malta. I had written down the frequencies for the radio beacons on Cap Bon and Cap Blanc in Tunisia and on Pantelleria Island in the strait between Sicily and Tunisia. Soon, we could expect to pick them up on the radio direction finder. But we needed that light on Marettimo to be sure we were well off the shoals.

"I got it," Doug said. "Bearing . . . " As he checked the direction with the hand-bearing compass, I stared into the darkness. The black water shimmered with deceptive moon glitter. I thought I saw three or four lights.

"Damn, it's gone," Doug said. "No . . . what the hell, there's another light, a couple of 'em."

"Hard to port," Malcolm sang out as he released the tiller lines to the wind vane and steered north. "There must be a mess of tuna nets out there."

An hour later we set course east for Marettimo again. The moon was higher now and it was easier to distinguish the horizon. After a few minutes we picked up the group-flashing light. As it only showed through a sector from 298 degrees to 151 degrees, we had been too far north to see it until the course change.

It was 0100 and still none of us wanted to sleep. When I went below to log our course change I measured off the distance to Marsala on the coast of Sicily, almost due east of Marettimo. Perhaps it was time for another day ashore.

"Marsala?" Mal said. "You drink that, don't you? Some kind of sweet wine."

"Yes, like sherry. I cook with it," I said. "I suppose this is where it comes from, like sherry from Jerez in Spain. Let's go sample some Marsala."

At dawn we had a hazy smudge of coast dead ahead to the west. The peak of Marettimo jutted out of clouds directly behind us. There were currents here, around the Egadian islands and Cap Boeo, but no obstacles. And now, we'd lost our wind. All day, we powered toward the miragelike coast, finally turning into the harbor in late afternoon.

Marsala was built on the typical Mediterranean pattern: a sheltered port guarded by a steep promontory. High medieval walls ringed the old city at the top of the limestone bluff. From the harbor, the town was a jumble of tile rooftops, brown parapets, and isolated spikes of palm trees. Television antennae spread across the buildings like some thorny, parasitic growth. We decided to skip a visit ashore that night and get some rest. *Matata* nestled alongside the low sea wall, again the only yacht in the harbor.

Mal and Doug were up before me and I heard them adjusting our lines ashore. But I was sure they didn't need my help, so I stayed curled in my sleeping bag, loath to rise so early. Mal peeked into the main cabin. "We'll go get some fresh bread and bacon," he said when he saw my eyes were open.

As I tidied up the cabin below, I felt the boat bump, crushing the fenders against the dock. Assuming it was a wake from a passing motorboat, I trusted in the fenders and returned to laying out our breakfast. It happened again. Then I heard the sickening sound of our gelcote topsides grinding against the rough stone. I was on deck in a second. We were being hurled against the sea wall by a sudden swell that rolled in the harbor mouth. As I thrust more fenders between the topsides and the wall, I grabbed for the boat hook. But I couldn't hold *Matata* off with it. As usual, I was barefoot, and the only way I could keep some distance from that wall was to sit on deck with my back jammed against the cabintop and push with my bare feet against the sharp stone as we rolled in for another grinding. Mal and Doug were nowhere in sight. At the foot of the quay was a grillwork gate that guarded the entrance to the medieval city of Marsala beyond the massive stone walls. The gate effectively kept casual strollers off the docks and there were no other boats near us to ask for help. It was just me and the boat and this damn swell.

I reviewed what I would have to do next if Mal and Doug didn't return soon. Dash down below and start the engine, fend off . . . release the spring lines, fend off . . . release the bow line but keep tension on it, tiller hard to starboard as I pulled in both fore and aft lines, *not* dropping them in the water to tangle around the prop, hope the transom didn't hit the wall before I could slip into forward gear. . . . And then, there I'd be circling around in the middle of the harbor waiting for my crew. Eventually, I'd have to come back in here to pick them up, come alongside alone, with this crazy swell.

When they were about 300 yards from the boat, I saw Mal break into a run. He must have wondered what was happening. From there he would have seen the mast wildly weaving back and forth, his wife seemingly trapped between the boat and the dock.

We quickly carried out the maneuver I had rehearsed in my mind, but much more easily with three people. Once safely off the dock, we had to decide what to do. First of all, there was an obvious change in the weather. The swell was coming from the south, straight into the mouth of the harbor. The sky exhibited all the nasty signs of a sirocco with cirro-stratus flicking long mare's tails toward us. And besides that, it looked like the whole fishing fleet of Sicily was suddenly trying to cram into the harbor—a sure sign of foul weather. Along the outer arm of the mole, the boats were maneuvering to raft up two and three deep, bows pointing into the swell—big wood-and-steel trawlers with high freeboards and ugly, dangerous-looking net rollers and davits poking out all over. Gingerly we approached one of the innermost groups and asked if we could come alongside them.

The three fishermen bunched up in the doghouse came out to take our lines. But how were we going to manage this, I wondered. *Matata* looked like a delicate tart shell next to these huge factory trawlers. We would have to tuck in under their net booms, keeping our topsides protected by fenders and trusting that our tall mast and shrouds swaying in the swell wouldn't get tangled up in the struts and poles jutting out from the trawler. It took the remainder of the morning, including three nearly disastrous attempts, before we finally snugged up to the trawler and felt reasonably sure that its protruding gear wouldn't sink us. We were the fourth boat out from the quay. These fishing trawlers were much higher than us, so I thought we were stuck out there for the duration of the storm; certainly, I'd never be able to make the ten-foot climb up to the trawler's rail.

And, in fact, we didn't leave the boat that day. The sirocco increased relentlessly. The barometer dropped from 30.80 to 30.52 in two hours. Gusts of wind and the terrific swell banged us around so that it took all three of us to fend off, constantly readjusting tension on the lines. At last, it rained . . . so we got wet too, but at least the wind began to drop.

"I think we should have kept going," I complained to Malcolm. "We'd be better off at sea."

He was tired and soaked through his layers of clothes. "Oh, yeah? You think we should be out there when all these guys," he gestured around at the fishing fleet, "are holing up here? That's shoal water south of here; it bunches up steeper and nastier than any sea you've ever seen. Just be glad we are in here."

I had to agree. We had luckily chosen the lesser of two evils. Odd as it seemed, I actually missed the days of Atlantic gales and endless sea room to run away from them.

Next morning, when the sirocco had abated somewhat, I insisted on trying to get ashore. After not bothering to top off the tanks in Carlo Forte, we were low on water, although there was plenty of food. If Doug and I took a couple of lug-a-jugs to the quay, I suggested, we could replenish the water supply. I badly wanted to be on firm land. This riding the swell in the harbor was making me seasick. Mal agreed, and with him giving me a shoulder to step on from *Matata*, and Doug up at the trawler rail pulling, I managed the climb. The three boats we scrambled over were chock full of coiled lines, thicker than anything on *Matata*, and long rows of nets laid out to dry. There were smelly baskets with bits of old dead fish melding with the diesel stench. Stray fish hooks caught at our jeans. The men on the boats nodded at us and gestured with friendly resignation at the low overcast and the swell. A smiling young fisherman pointed out the best way to get from one boat to another.

Once ashore, we learned that there was no water point nearby. Assuming there would be a water fountain and spigot in the town square, as in most Mediterranean cities, we trudged toward town. It was a long way, but it felt wonderful to be on *terra firma*, although the land seemed to be moving under my feet. I noticed I wasn't walking a very straight line after so many days on a moving boat.

A shiny red Fiat trailed us for a few moments, then stopped next to us. The man got out and offered to give us a ride. "I help you," he insisted in English. He said he was called Gianni and everyone knew him. In the end he drove us to the main water point on the other side of the harbor where the ferries came in; we filled our jugs and he drove us back.

Now, a Sicilian with a car who speaks some English is not

someone you should offer to tip, I reasoned. So, I invited him to visit *Matata* and join us for a cup of coffee. With his help, we lugged our water jugs over the three fishing boats and descended to *Matata*.

Gianni was about thirty-five, darkly handsome but rawboned, his nose broken, his ears ripply with white scar tissue. His kind manner and a smile that flashed white, broken teeth was very appealing. When Gianni climbed off *Matata* he suggested that we all come that evening to his restaurant. He wanted to show us around Marsala.

The storm had abated enough by evening to allow us to leave the boat. After a driving tour around the outskirts of the old walled city, Gianni pressed us to visit his home. He lived in a modern, three-floor apartment building in a rubbly industrial suburb. There were several rooms off a dim entrance hall. The one into which he lead us was crowded with the uncomfortable, overstuffed furniture and massive armoires fashionable among the middle classes in Italy. We were given Johnnie Walker Black Label whisky to drink out of large, cut-glass tumblers. Malcolm commented on the pictures scattered around the room showing a younger Gianni in boxer's trunks, his taped fists held high.

"I box many years. One time in America. Elizabeth, New Jersey . . . Newark." With this, we were treated to an album of photos and newspaper cuttings spanning his career.

Gianni's wife and two children were paraded before us but slipped out to the kitchen as soon as it was polite. Then, we were off in the car again, bouncing along unlit, cobbled streets. "His" restaurant meant that he frequented it, not that he owned it, we discovered. Malcolm asked him his profession, what work he did now that his career in the ring was over. But Gianni was evasive. Either he did nothing for a living (not likely, given the new car and apartment), or he just wasn't telling. With practiced skill, he circumvented any direct question. Later we realized that Gianni was probably a Mafioso sent to "protect" us. There was a strange ethical code at work here that we could not easily fathom. We were stormbound in a Sicilian port, literally at the mercy of the elements. If we were robbed or molested in any way, this might reflect badly on the local *capo*. Thus, we needed protection. Apparently, Gianni's presence on the quay had been no accident.

In the three days we were holed up in Marsala, we left the boat unattended several times, unlocked and with all sorts of gear on deck, well in sight of any potential thief. But nothing was touched. I like to think that our trusting nature elicited this respectful response from the fishermen. But, more likely, Gianni's presence warned that there would be hell to pay if these foreigners were harmed in any way.

At last the weather broke, the swell dropped in the harbor, and we moved *Matata* back alongside the sea wall. Mal and I took the opportunity to go ashore the simple way, crossing the foot of water with one small leap. For two hours that last afternoon in Marsala we walked, stretching the muscles of our calves that stiffened when we were at sea or confined to the boat a long while. We circled the high walls on the sea side of the city. These walls had been built to ward off the attacks of Saracen pirates and assorted conquerers over the centuries and looked like they could still do the job. Gazing down from Cap Boeo, we saw the Egadian islands strewn at our feet. Although the sea had calmed a bit, there was still surf beating on their southern shores from the residual swell. In any case, we knew the weather was improving, because all morning the fishing boats had been peeling off from the pack and heading back out there, to that narrow, shallow strait that lay to the south, to set their nets for the fish that provided their livelihood. Tomorrow, we would join them.

The southeast wind had finally dropped. I stood in the piazza at the end of the cobbled street that curved down to the harbor. Carol had asked me to pick up some tomatoes and any fresh fruit I could find on my way back from the bank. But I had almost left the meager shopping district when I remembered the errand, and now I had to double back to the small greengrocer at the other end of the square.

I hesitated, one foot on the broken curb, the other in the street.

Above the chipped façades of the houses, wide rips of blue sky were opening in the overcast. From here I could see ten miles out to sea. The swell was down to manageable proportions, and there was no white water. It was just past noon, time for us to be under way. Already we'd lost three days, stormbound in Marsala.

I hated to waste more time. My impatience was in part due to the creaking pace of the formalities I'd had to complete at the harbor master's office and the bank. All morning, I'd been either sitting on splayed wooden benches or standing on the cold stone floor of some functionary's grandiose office, waiting for the official to affix yet one more rubber stamp to the portfolio of documents I'd been obliged to lug around.

At the Banco d'Italia, the task of reconverting 30,000 lire to dollars had proceeded at a stately pace, as I was dispatched from one counter to the next, then on to a series of massive oak desks, behind which scowling clerks waited to review every character of text, every numeral and digit of this minor transaction. Once again, I was forced to recognize how insular Marsala was and, for that matter, the whole island of Sicily. They did not get many tourists here, certainly not in this season. With the exception of our unofficial escort, Gianni, our other dealings with the townspeople had been marked by a censorious distance, a thinly hidden disapproval on the part of the shopkeepers and restaurant waiters. This emotion hadn't shown itself in active dislike or rudeness, but I knew that they'd all be happy to see the last of us. We were *stranieri*, outsiders.

As I hurried across the sunny square, I noticed groups of children watching from the shady, arched entranceways of their buildings. Silent, motionless, their faces empty, only their eyes active. I had been a foreigner among curious children on five of the world's continents, but I'd never before encountered such cool, static scrutiny. Usually, kids were a reasonably pleasant nuisance that a foreigner in Leopoldville, Tehran, or Saigon simply had to accept. Children called to you; they tried to shine your shoes or sell you chewing gum. Sometimes they begged; sometimes they pandered. But the kids here were like watchful old peasants. Distrust and distaste of foreigners masked their faces and dampened their normal kinetic play. When they saw us coming, they'd drop their rubber balls and quietly retreat to doorways to observe our passing.

Slowly, I was coming to understand this prevailing attitude. Sicily was definitely "insular"; the term was, after all, derived from the Latin *insula*, an island. And the island of Sicily, the largest in the Med, had been invaded, ravaged, pillaged, occupied, ruled, and generally mistreated by practically every civilization contending for supremacy in this region since the beginnings of recorded history. Even before that, organized myth—the *Odyssey*—had ample comment on Sicilians' feelings about visiting mariners.

For thirty-five centuries, armed, aggressive foreigners had been coming here in boats, determined to cut themselves in on the island's agricultural and mineral bounty or to seize its strategic harbors and use Sicily as a springboard for grander invasions. Ports like Marsala had been unwilling hosts to Phoenicians, the armies of warring Greek cities, Carthaginians, Republican and Imperial Roman fleets, Saracens, Goths, Vandals, Byzantines, medieval Venetians, Lombards . . . the list was long, extending well into modern times. And during all these turbulent, bloody centuries, the local people had been forced to bow under the domination of superior strength.

Although few locals would have acknowledged the psychological roots of their xenophobia, there was probably also a sexual component to their feelings about outsiders. After all, the invading hoards, from Ionian warriors in triremes to American GIs aboard LSTs, had been male soldiers. They raped and prostituted the native women, once they had gotten the serious business of killing out of the way. During these thousands of years, the fleets and armies that had occupied Sicily had left behind their obvious genetic contribution. The Sicilians, like Cretans, Maltese, Mallorcans, and *tanjaoui*, were a hybrid race, the product of the various tides of invasion that had swept across their communities.

Deep down, at the murky level of collective, archetypical fear, the Sicilians no doubt *knew* that they carried the bastard genes of the pagan Greeks, the Goths, and the Saracens. The shame and distaste of sexual domination colored their attitudes toward strangers and governed their elaborate and rigid moral code. A villager might murder a rival in a clan feud and suffer no legal prosecution. But any Sicilian who seduced an opponent's wife, a sister or daughter—or had the unspeakable audacity to rape a man's *mother*—would bring down the unified wrath of the community upon him.

The distrust extended to the Sicilians' Italian compatriots, not only to foreigners. At one point in our conversation with Gianni the night before, I had mentioned the terrorists of the Red Brigade and the fact that Carol and I had known several young Brigade sympathizers when we'd lived near Trieste four years earlier. Were the *brigati* a problem here in Sicily? I asked.

Gianni adopted an expression of barely patient tolerance, shaking his head with ponderous motion. "Bah," he said, "they know better than to come here, to *Sicilia*. We watch every outsider, every *straniero* who gets off the boat. If some *brigatisto* was stupid enough to come, he would be dead the next morning." He offered his lupine smile and did a chilling pantomime, his cocked thumb and forefinger forming the barrel of a gun held against the head of a kneeling figure. "They would find him in the gutter when they clean the street."

The greengrocer's shop was, as the saying goes, poor but clean. He had a chipped marble counter, three whitewashed walls strung with chains of garlic and dried red peppers, and a rusty iron grate that he could lock across the open storefront when he went home at night. His produce was displayed in splintery crates that looked like they had been salvaged from Garibaldi's quartermaster. As I approached the counter, the old fellow turned away, offering me the back of his dusty black suitcoat.

He made a show of straightening some crates, then bent to retrieve flecks of carrot stem from the clean stone floor. Clearly, he was not eager to deal with me face to face.

"*Bon giorno, signore,*" I called, as cheerfully as I could to his blank back.

He nodded, a slight dip of his close-cropped gray head, in recognition of my greeting.

In two days of shopping with this old man, I'd not managed to elicit a verbal response. At first I'd thought he was a deaf mute, but then I'd heard him talking with some black-shawled old crone when I'd come up here during a lull in the sirocco, our second afternoon in Marsala.

The hell with him I thought, and selected several ripe tomatoes. He had a couple of nice-looking pears and one firm green melon, obviously the last of this season's harvest. I placed my selection next to his archaic brass counterweight scale and waited for the old man to act. Moving slowly, with the reluctance of a condemned prisoner about to face the firing squad, the old grocer finally turned to the front of his shop. But he kept his eyes down while he ponderously weighed each of my purchases. As he worked, I studied his thick, arthritic fingers, the gray stubble of his cheeks, the gold-framed spectacles, one bow patched with wire. There was no hostility in this old man, only embarrassed discomfort in the presence of a foreigner. I smiled as warmly as I could and hoped he could see me above the lenses of his glasses.

If he did, he was unable to acknowledge the gesture. He verified his penciled addition and thrust the scrap of brown paper toward me. The total was 1,200 lire, less than a dollar. Carefully, I laid a 1,000-lire bill on the counter and stacked four fifty-lire coins beside it.

"*Va bene?*" I asked.

He nodded without speaking.

I slid the fruit into my string bag and lay the tomatoes carefully on top. "*Andiamo òggi,*" I said in an almost conversational tone. "*Andiamo nel Malta . . . mille grazie per tutti.*" My Italian was almost as rudimentary as my Spanish, but I thought he might respond.

Slowly, the dusty black shoulder turned away once more. The gray head dipped without speaking.

I was ten paces into the sunny piazza when the old man called. "Meester . . . meester *capitano.*"

When I turned, he was beside me, holding out a bright yellow lemon, the size and texture of his gnarled fist. "*Per la signora,*" he said, smiling now with dark, crumbling teeth. "*Bonviaggio, meester capitano.*"

I took the gift, then shook the old man's leathery hand. Behind his glasses, his eyes were young and lively. "*Òggi,*" he said, "*fa bel tempo.*"

Strolling down the cobbled road to the port, the string bag of produce in one hand, my plastic document folder in the other, I experienced a powerful sense of pleasure, of harmony. We were sailing through a civilization, I realized, not simply a sea bounded by capes and shoals. And now, after the old grocer's responsive gesture of friendship, I felt that we had managed to touch the human flesh of that complex civilization.

We tied up alongside the greasy Marsala cargo dock, opposite the sea wall where we'd ridden out the sirocco. This was the only water point in the harbor, and I wanted to top off our tanks and lug-a-jugs with clean spring water. I'd heard bad things about both the quality and availability of water in Malta, and I didn't wish to be delayed there before our long passage across the Ionian to Greece. I was still pleased by my encounter with the old shopkeeper, and I felt no impatience at having to wait for the water hose while the long blue tuna trawler filled her tanks, prior to sailing for the banks off Tunisia. Most of the fleet had already departed that morning, a clear indication to me that the storm was over and that we were in for several days of good weather, just like the old man had told me.

Carol was off on a final errand, and Doug and I sat in the sunny cockpit, chatting about nothing of import while, just ahead of us on the pier, the trawler crew went through their jovial and boisterous routine of coiling tackle and stacking fish crates. About half this crew were Italians, I saw, and half North African, dark Arabs and Maghribi Berbers with blue eyes and curly auburn hair.

One Arab kid about eighteen wandered over to look at *Matata*. He was barefoot and shirtless in the warm afternoon sun, his counterfeit Levi's rolled up to the knee. After appraising our furled sails, deck gear, and rigging, he strolled aft along the hot concrete pier to stare at the plywood wind vane. I recognized the boy's mixed curiosity and native reserve. He wanted to ask us what that weird device was, but he was too polite to bluntly question such obviously wealthy *ensarra.*

I took the plunge. *"Seba'l hir,"* I tried in my best Maghrebi accent. The boy's smile was sudden, complete. *"Seba'l hir, a sidi,"* he responded, then cut loose a stream of high-speed Arabic far beyond my comprehension.

I smiled back, but held up my right hand to stop him. *"Vous parlez français?"* I asked. *"Nous ne parlons pas beaucoup d'arab."*

Again he beamed. *"Mais, certainement, m'sieu. Je suis de la Tunisie. J'ai fait la lycée, moi."*

As we talked, I quickly realized that his mild boast about completing Tunisian secondary school was a fib, but I couldn't blame the kid for exaggerating. His name was Abdelkader and he came from a village near Sfax, a long way from the sea. For the past two years, he said, he'd been working as a deckhand on this trawler, sending all his money home to his *"papa et maman"* in Tunisia. The job was hard, he admitted, but in Tunisia, there was no work whatsoever.

We showed him the boat and traced our route from Gibraltar on the big Mediterranean Sea chart. Doug gave him a warm Coke, and I explained that we hadn't been able to get any ice here.

"La glace vient d'une usine très loins," he explained gravely, frowning at our dilemma as if it were somehow his problem too.

We heard the trawler's big diesels rumble to life, and Abdelkader rejoined his crew to cast off. Just as the fishing boat was beginning to pull off the pier, dead slow ahead, Abdelkader appeared at the wide taffrail, clutching a plastic sack and waving his free hand. Doug rushed up to the bow to grab the dripping sack before it fell into the water. The Arab boy waved once more, shouting, *"Bon chance et bon voyage."*

Swinging carefully aft with the clumsy sack, Doug grinned warmly. "Check this out," he said.

There were two milky white blocks of ice in the sack and two icy green bottles of Heineken beer.

Doug opened the beers with his Swiss Army knife and we raised the bottles in a toast to Abdelkader. The trawler thumped and chugged, backing and turning in the narrow harbor, then dug in its heels and trundled out past the sea wall, smacking into the leftover swell. At the rusty stern net roller, Abdelkader smiled in the sunlight, waving with both hands above his head. The sky was hard blue. Above us, the sun pounded silently on the brown walls of the ancient city.

CHAPTER EIGHT

OCTOBER 16, 0200
MALTA CHANNEL

I wiped the dew off the starboard cockpit cushion and sat down to take the tiller from Carol. Around us, the night sea and sky were indistinguishable, a black void, lacking shape or texture. The overcast masked the stars and moon, the sea was flat, free of phosphorescence. Off to port, the white range lights of a large, fast tanker marched toward us out of the night, silent, inanimate as a computer simulation. More ships moved behind us, abstractions of white and colored lights.

Carol slumped for a moment, rubbing the fatigue from her face. In the glow of the compass lamp she looked old and worn, beaten down to a nub by the past twenty-four hours. I knew that I did not look any better. Finally, she spoke. "I didn't have any trouble holding one-fifty," she nodded toward the compass. "The shipping's passing on either side of us. I guess they can see our masthead light all right."

Her voice was neutral, emotionless. She was in no mood to sit there and keep me company as she usually did when I relieved her late-night watch. Obviously, she was still rankled by the bitter acrimony we had exchanged since leaving Marsala.

I reached out to touch her arm. "Get some sleep," I said quietly. "I'll take it until five, then Doug can do three hours. We'll be off Valletta by then."

She stiffened under my touch. "I'm okay. Just stand your regular watches." She rose unsteadily and swung forward. "We *all* need rest."

She was gone below. No light showed from the cabin, and I guessed that she had simply collapsed on her bunk and was sleeping in her clothes, a wise enough precaution. All the way down the coast of Sicily, I'd had to interrupt her sleep when the weather turned on us, or when I'd needed her advice about changing course. Hopefully, that fiasco of headwinds and indecision, followed by exhausted argument, was behind us.

After checking out of Marsala, we had beat our way into the inevitable easterly breeze and used up all our daylight and half the night making our way along Sicily's southern coast, so that we could turn southeast and lay Malta, close-hauled, on the port tack. Diabolically, the breeze shifted on us within an hour of our course change. The wind also rose to a nasty 25 knots, and the short sea began to hump up in this shallow channel. Malta was only forty-six miles ahead, but, given this wind, I knew that we'd have to sail twice that distance, beating down there.

An English charter skipper friend in Rhodes had once managed to raise the spirits of his crew and guests who were demoralized by incessant meltemi headwinds by mounting the following message prominently above his chart table:

Definition of Apparent Wind:
Apparent Wind = Intended Course $+/-$ .00001°

But the nasty joke that the wind was playing on us south of Sicily had not elicited any laughter from the crew of *Matata*. For three hours we pounded and smacked, making little headway in the current. Doug and I had reefed and changed down to the working jib. We'd tried the starboard tack to work our way further east, but, with devilish precision the wind had backed around to head us. Naturally, it veered right back on our nose when we tacked again to a southeast course. To compound our problems, the barometer was falling fast —just as it had in Marsala—and the sky had completely clouded over.

Soaked with spray, aching tired, and worried about another sirocco catching us out in this relatively shallow channel, I called Carol from her bunk and told her we'd better turn around and seek temporary shelter in the fishing harbor of Porto Empedocle. She was so groggy that she agreed without much discussion. We tacked northwest, reset the genoa, and rolled, banging and clattering down the swell, for the rest of the night, each hour taking us six nautical miles *away* from our goal.

That afternoon we all slept poorly in the filthy, crowded little artificial harbor the Italian government built at the ancient port of Agrigento, which had been bombed into rubble in World War II. Trawlers and mackerel smacks came and went all around us, accompanied by the usual shouts and histrionics of Mediterranean fishermen trying to impress foreign yacht sailors. That night we had to shift our mooring, *twice,* as huge white car ferries shouldered their way into the narrow port. The next morning the sky was clear, the wind gentle from the northeast. The threatened sirocco, on which I had based my decision to seek shelter in this unfortunate sanctuary, had never materialized.

We sailed just before noon, having been again delayed by the glacial bureaucracy of Italian port authorities. Ten miles out, after we had experimented with different combinations of sail and heading, it became clear that the northeast breeze blowing across Porto Empedocle was a local phenomenon. Out here in the sloppy, vestigial swell, there was no wind whatsoever. So we were back in the same quandary as the previous day: fifty miles from Malta with no decent wind to take us there. We decided to power at fast cruising speed with the mainsail set to steady the boat.

But after I'd had the chance to study the charts again, I began to formulate another plan. Why not, I suggested, skip Malta altogether, and simply swing east to power right past Sicily and into the southern Ionian en route to Crete? Doug responded very well to this change of plans. But Carol did not like the idea at all. She hunched over the chart table in her rumpled, salt-stiff sweatshirt and jeans, frowning at the course and distance figures I'd scrawled on a yellow pad.

"Okay," she finally muttered, "I can see how we'd save a day or two by skipping Malta. But what about the mail we've had forwarded there?" Her voice rose. "What about the check? Did you just decide to skip *that*, too?"

Sarcasm or bitter invective were not part of Carol's normal repertoire. Her resorting to this tone now was a clear sign that the emotional hassle of trying to complete this trip on an unrealistic budge was affecting her.

I tried to reason. "Honey, listen a second." I paused, searching for the right phrases that would not make her more defensive. "We have no way of knowing if they even sent that check to Gibraltar. If they *did*, we can't be sure that the harbor master in Gib forwarded it to Malta. Christ . . . " I waved my hands in frustration. "You know how these people are. They probably sent the check back to New York when we didn't stick around to pick it up in Gib. I think we should just press on to Greece and sort things out there."

Carol's neck and shoulders were set, rigid. She did not look at me when she answered. "Now *you* listen for a minute." She leaned back to make sure Doug was at the rear of the cockpit, outside of hearing range. "We have less than two hundred dollars left. If we have to keep using the engine so much, we won't have enough money for both diesel fuel and food. We *need* that check. You have to realize . . . "

The combination of fatigue, disappointment with the weather, and money anxiety had gotten to me, too. "Goddamn it," I shouted. "I'm well aware of our money situation. Sailing down to Malta on some wild damned goose chase for that check is not going to improve the situation. We should cut our losses and just sail for Greece. We don't need diesel fuel if we're out in open water. We can sail, for Christ's sake . . . this is a *sailboat*, in case you've forgotten."

Her face was congested, hot red with anger. "And what if the check's sitting down there right now? Seven thousand dollars, sitting in an envelope in the port captain's office? Do you seriously think the publisher will just issue another check and send it off to Lindos because we tell them we can't find the first one they mailed?" She bunched her fists and thrust my yellow pad away from her. "You're just acting stupid . . . selfish, like you always do when you've already made up your mind to do something."

I grabbed the yellow pad and ripped it into three ragged pieces, sacrificing half our remaining supply of navigation note stock in the childish process. "All right!" I yelled. "We'll do it your way. Just don't . . . "

Carol rose and pushed her way past me, interrupting my nasty tirade. She slammed the swaying accordion door to the main cabin and lashed it shut. I couldn't be sure, but, over the thumping of the engine, I thought I heard her crying.

The large tanker stalked toward us in the black night. Now I could see his red portside running light. After a few minutes, his range lights cast wavering white tracks on the greasy surface of the swell, and I was able to gain a sense of dimension for the first time since taking the watch. The kettledrum rumble of the tanker's engines reached me, melding with the endless idiot thump of our own diesel. It was almost three, and I didn't feel sleepy. I decided to let Doug have an extra hour; I'd call him at 0500 and let Carol sleep in, despite her earlier request to be called at six.

I was not being magnanimous, I realized, simply cautious. Another bitter exchange while both of us were exhausted might provoke real problems. But I knew that she'd be in a better mood once she'd had six full hours of sleep. Besides, I mused, I was actually enjoying the slow-motion Star Wars interplay of the calm black channel and the ships' range lights. I leaned back against the cushion and sipped my cool coffee. The Malta channel, I knew, was a truly historic body of water. At that very moment, I was sailing above the graves of thousands of sailors.

I had first become interested in Malta when I'd met old John Calvert, the owner of *Buscador,* a converted Cornish trawler that always summered in Lindos bay in the early 1970s. John was retired Royal Navy, an engineer who had risen from petty officer to commander during forty years at sea. He lived alone aboard the lumbering fifty-ton trawler, his only companions the BBC World Service and a little mongrel bitch named Trixie. If I were a casting agent trying to fill roles in the film adaptations of Conrad's novels, I'd keep John Calvert's address handy. Barrel-chested and bald, with long, muscular arms and fingers like blunt tool bits, John could repair any piece of broken nautical gear you brought him, from an outboard motor to a bent anchor.

During what are now called the "dark days" early in World War II, John found himself reassigned to destroyers in the Med, an exciting enough line of work. But in the autumn of 1941, while on a refit in Gibraltar, John learned of an even more interesting assignment. The navy needed experienced officers to lead volunteer crews aboard cargo vessels attempting to break the naval and aerial blockade of Malta and replenish the island.

Malta was surrounded by Axis forces; the German Afrika Korps and Luftwaffe and the Italian Navy and Air Force held the North African coast and Sicily. Their U-boats and destroyers dominated the surrounding waters. For months, the harbors, towns, and dockyards of Malta were pounded by almost hourly air raids. It was clear to all concerned that the island would fall if it weren't resupplied with munitions, fuel, and food. John Calvert's volunteer assignment found him in command of a small coastal tanker of indiscriminate pedigree and vintage, laden with a thousand tons of high-octane aviation gasoline. His wardroom consisted of polyglot volunteer officers, and the fo'c'sle housed Chinese refugee sailors under the rule of a tough Hong Kong bosun.

Captain Calvert completed three runs to Malta during the Axis siege. The convoys in which he sailed averaged loss rates of 75 percent; some suffered only 50 percent casualties; others simply disappeared from the face of the sea. During the two and one-half years that Malta was under siege, scores of ships went to the bottom of the shallow strait. When the Axis occupation of North Africa collapsed, and Marshall Kesserling tried to extract the Afrika Korps and its Italian allies from Tunisia, hundreds of vessels—the bulk of the evacuation fleet—were sunk in these waters, many by RAF bombers flying from fields in Malta.

The tiny Maltese archipelago and its surrounding channels had a bloody history, even by the martial standards of the Mediterranean. Like Sicily to the north, Malta lay in an extremely strategic position, a cork in the slender bottleneck dividing the eastern and western Med. Ever since the days when Phoenician merchants controlled the Middle Sea twenty-five hundred years ago, admirals had realized the importance of Malta. On its southeast coast, Malta had several deep natural harbors that provided ample shelter for a merchant fleet and squadrons of warships. Any naval power controlling Malta eventually dominated the commerce that transited the Mediterranean. Without control of Malta, no navy could be secure in the surrounding waters—as the Axis powers discovered in 1943. Malta had been the key to Britain's Mediterranean strategy from the Napoleonic wars until the 1960s. Before the British, the Knights of Saint John ruled Malta and used the islands as their base to challenge and ultimately block the expansion of the Ottoman Empire.

As we powered along through the thick, gently rolling darkness, our keel passed above the wrecks of Carthaginian and Greek triremes, Roman grain ships, Venetian galleys, the *carracks* of the Knights, and siege ships of Sulieman the Magnificent. There were caravels of Barbary pirates down there, two hundred feet beneath us. Some of Nelson's frigates rested on that limestone bottom, beside the hulks of U-boats, liberty ships, and Wellington bombers. Throughout history, men had journeyed from Europe, Africa, and Asia to kill each other in, under, and above these calm, dark waters.

Ironically, I knew, their bones and the wreckage of their vessels now lay intermingled with the remains of Europe's earliest human inhabitants. This shallow strait separating North Africa from Sicily and the mainland of Europe had not always been a water barrier between the two continents. As recently as ten thousand years ago, at the end of the last glacial period, the rolling plains and valleys that now composed the naval cemetery beneath us were the lush grazing ranges of antelope, bison, wild sheep, and other assorted Pleistocene fauna.

Among the predators who followed these herds north were clans of Cro-Magnon hunters. Their cave drawings, flint tools, and horn speartips can be found in abundance in Malta and nearby Gozo, as well as in grave sites on Lampedusa and other isolated islets that compose the remnants of the submerged land bridge between Europe and Africa. Anthropologists now believe that Europe's "indigenous" populations advanced and retreated across this land bridge in cycles that followed the ebb and flood of the continental ice sheets. During the Ice Ages, the Sahara was a lush veldt, and Paleolithic hunters thrived. Cave paintings in present-day Mauritania and Mali are as lustrous and evocatively haunting as any found in the limestone caves of the Pyrenees.

It is now impossible to plot with any certainty exactly when and where the Stone Age hunters crossed the land bridge, but it has been well established that the bridge existed. Just as the Aleutian archipelago provided a land route for Stone Age Asians to cross into North America and eventually, through repeated waves of migration, to people the western hemisphere, the Sicily-Malta-Lampedusa bridge allowed the Pleistocene ancestors of the Finns, Magyars, and Basques—who are all linguistically related—to advance north when the climate began to moderate.

Given the murky cross-currents of cause and effect during the prehistoric millennia, I mused, watching the ships' lights on the dark water, it might well be true that Malta was more strategic than any modern historians suspected. If the local geology had differed slightly and the land bridge had not existed, the ethnic composition of Europe would have also differed at the time of the great Celtic and Urnfield migrations. Possibility for speculation was rich, but the exercise was eventually futile. Europe's history was, I knew, a function of its people, barbarian and civilized. In turn, the ethnic composition of its people was a function of climate and geology. *We're here because we're here because . . .*

I rigged the tiller lines and ducked down to the galley to make another cup of coffee and stage a barbarian raid of my own on the tin box of Danish cookies. We had bought four boxes of these expensive sweets from Sacconee and Speed in Gibraltar. This was the last box. Naturally, giving up Danish butter cookies for the remainder of the trip would not represent a real hardship. But I had to face the unpleasant fact that our remaining $189 did not represent a very big cash reserve for the rest of the trip. We still had seven hundred miles of Mediterranean to cross before we were home free in Lindos, where we could charge our cookies and frozen hamburger and tomato juice at Tsampiko Pallas's grocery store while we traced the whereabouts of our missing check.

Back in the cockpit, I squinted at the compass, then closed my eyes to restore my night vision after the flashlight glare down in the galley. When I opened my eyes again, I saw that stars were beginning to sparkle out ahead of us. I watched intently as the eastern horizon acquired a flat black edge. Even though there was no surface wind, the dark overcast was rolling back overhead, like a curtain from a skylight. All across the sky, the stars blinked on. The sea around the boat took on the faint sheen of starlight.

Half an hour later, the sky was clear, satiny black, swarming with cold stars. More ships passed on either side of our track, to and from Suez and the oil ports of the Middle East, carrying crude petroleum to Europe and consumer goods to Jiddah and the gulf. Our diesel engine throbbed and rumbled, the exhaust bubbling in the quarter wave, just below my left elbow. Despite the coffee, a dark weight of sleep had settled on my shoulders. I stood and yawned deeply, then did a sloppy little jig, my bare feet slipping on the dewy gelcoat, to restore my circulation and wake me up. It was no good. Sleep pulled me down, like a warm, wet cape. My eyes glued, and my face dropped to brush the damp folds of my windbreaker.

I woke in an instant, aware that the boat was swinging off to port, toward the bow of a low-slung coastal freighter. This wouldn't do. After I called Doug, I leaned over the starboard rail and splashed cool sea water in my face. Normally, this would shock me out of a sleepy stupor. Tonight, the water only seemed to increase my torpor. By the time Doug had dressed, consulted the chart, read the log, and made himself a cup of coffee, I was slumped on the starboard cushion, only partly conscious of the compass course that an autonomous region of my nervous system was somehow steering. He took the helm, commented on what a pretty night it was, and I sank into sleep, curled like a child on the short cockpit bench.

When he called me, his voice sounded as if it came through an echoing, humid cave. Peach sky and blue shell-smooth water appeared as I raised myself to both elbows. Doug looked cold and tired at the helm, squinting against the faint sheen of the early dawn. Ponderously, I let one leg and then the other drop into the cockpit well, stretched, and shook my head.

"Malta," Doug said, nodding toward the starboard bow. "At least I *think* it is."

I stood and again stretched my limbs and back. What I saw ahead of us did not at first seem logical, or even possible. Stooping again, I splashed water across my eyes and rubbed my face, hard, with the calloused heels of my hands.

I grabbed the binoculars and studied the island. The tan mass rose abruptly from the geometrically flat sheet of pale water. Twisting the focus knob, I scanned the land again, from the low, honey-colored mound nearest us to the darker jumble away to the southeast. Through an optical quirk provoked by the angle of the early sun, the unusually clear atmosphere, and the utterly calm sea, we could now see Malta and Gozo in great detail. I estimated our distance at fifteen miles, which meant the highlands of the islands hung above the limits of the nautical horizon. It was just before six, and their limestone cliffs in ridges caught the first direct sunlight, while here the surface of the sea was still somber with retreating night.

But, I realized, whatever the causes for this optical phenomenon, the end result was bizarre, almost frightening. As we chugged along through the still dawn, the two islands rose from the sea as if they were part of some mythical, submerged continent in a low-budget Japanese monster movie. Ten minutes later, I could see the narrow channel that separated the smaller island of Gozo to the north from the dry, tan bulk of Malta. There should have been an even smaller island called Comino in the channel, but I couldn't yet distinguish it.

What I could see, however, remained illogical, alien to anything I'd seen before. The islands were brown and treeless, with naked rock escarpments and cliff faces along the eastern coasts. Through the binoculars, I could easily identify the weathered limestone and occasional scrub brush of the Sahara. But it was not the desert island landscape that was troubling. I'd been a Peace Corps director in Mauritania, and the images of the summer Sahara would remain in my memory as long as I lived.

There was this strange *city* out there covering half of Malta, not a tile-roofed Mediterranean village, not the usual arrangement of whitewashed port, the *scala* surmounted by the sanctuary of the upper town within its medieval walls . . . none of the normal visual cues were there. Instead, a full-blown *Mittel Europa* city of dense stone buildings, church spires, apartment blocks, and massive government edifices—all evocative of Belgrade or Budapest—marched across the bare, dessicated rock of the island, covering fully half its surface as seen from this perspective. It was as if a nineteenth century burg had been uprooted from the Austro-Hungarian Empire and deposited on this naked limestone ridge. Clearly, I was looking at two distinct, unrelated entities: the city and the desert island. From this angle and distance, there did not appear to be any organic connection between the two. The city simply stopped about halfway along the stony ridge . . . no suburbs, not a shed or chicken coop visible, just brown rock.

I dragged up the chart and spread it on the closed hatch to get a better idea of the scale and perspective of what we saw. Valletta and Sliema were marked as one continuous city, stretching from the southeast cape of the island about eight miles along the seventeen-mile coastline. The urban area did not extend very far inland, but on our approach angle we couldn't see that. From the cockpit of *Matata*, Malta appeared to be a skillfully contrived set from a science-fiction film, a city half-vaporized by some death ray, so that all remnants of the devastated section had disappeared, leaving behind a desert void.

If I squinted, the sci-fi perspective still held. But now, Malta became the dust-jacket illustration from a lurid space wars epic, a naked, lifeless asteroid onto which an ancient city had been transmigrated by some evil genius with a name like Throtan or Bloroc.

I handed Doug the binoculars. "Have a look at *that.*"

He focused and stared through the glasses, then cleaned the lenses. Again he tried various degrees of focus and magnification. "Looks like the city's just *stuck* on there, like it dropped out of the sky or something."

Passing him the chart, I tried to explain the optical phenomenon. Doug frowned at the damp sheet and squinted up at Malta. "Still weird," he muttered. "That's just too big a city for such a little damn island."

I gazed up again at the dense ranks of buildings, the domes and archways of the larger structures, then along the dry cliffs of the western coast. *Weird* was Doug's epithet. I could not think of a better one.

By eight-thirty, we were a mile off Salina Bay, sailing now in a cool northerly breeze beneath the towering natural and manmade ramparts of greater Valletta. Carol was awake, fresh and cheerful in shorts and a bright summer blouse, fully rested, as if the angry muddle of the night had never occurred. We sat in the breezy shade of the mainsail, gazing at the fortifications that opened up ahead of us.

Now we could see the entrance to Valletta's Grand Harbour. At the end of a steep, fortified promontory stood Fort Saint Elmo, a star-shaped Renaissance bastion with massive brown limestone walls. This point divided the two deep bays, Grand Harbour and Marsamxett Creek. From the fort, the limestone ramparts stretched along both sides of the promontory, a thick, protective shield that had been almost continuously improved since the sixteenth century, to transform the steep hillsides of the natural anchorages into towering curtain walls, broken at intervals by strong points and bastions. I had seen most of the walled cities of medieval and Renaissance Europe. These fortifications made them seem the work of amateurs.

Behind the ramparts rose tiers of pale golden stone buildings, some with arched porticoes and grand arcades of balconies facing the harbor. At this distance, I could see that my earlier impression of a stolid *Mittel Europa* city had been false. Valletta and its neighbor Sliema now appeared architecturally related more to medieval Jerusalem and the other *outre mer* cities of the crusaders in the Levant. This, of course, made good sense. Valletta had been built by Jean de La Vallette, Grand Master of the Knights of Saint John of Jerusalem.

We were sailing beneath the ramparts of Fort Saint Elmo, and I moved to the port rail to get a better view of the strong point. Although the thick walls were pitted and gouged here and there with unrepaired bomb damage, the bastion appeared basically sound, convincingly impregnable. This was, I knew, an illusion. Fort Saint Elmo had, in fact, fallen to the Turkish forces during the great Ottoman siege of 1565. That long battle and the heroic defense of this fort represented one of the most important military campaigns in European history.

The siege of Malta by the Ottoman Sultan, Sulieman the Magnificent, and his famous admiral, Barbarossa, was the highwater mark of Turkish penetration into what Winston Churchill later called "the soft underbelly of Europe." Barbarossa went on to conquer most of North Africa from the Arab Muslim caids who collectively misruled that territory. But the Turks were never able to capture a bridgehead and expand into the heart of Renaissance Europe. Once again, Malta proved itself to be the cork in the strategic bottleneck of the Central Mediterranean.

The failure of the great siege of Malta was not due to any lack of bravery or organization on the part of Sulieman's forces. In fact, his complex and meticulously ordered amphibious operation served as an instructional model for such endeavors in European military academies for three centuries. It was the desperate tenacity of the Knights, their European auxiliaries, and the Christian population of Malta that eventually broke the back of the Turkish siege. For almost five months in the baking summer of 1565, nine thousand Christian knights and soldiers repulsed the repeated assaults of 30,000 elite Turkish troops. Sulieman brought his best artillerymen and siege guns with him to Malta, as well as the cream of his Janizaries, the imperial guard of Christian converts who had lead the successful sieges of Budapest and Belgrade.

But before this impressive force could encircle and attack de La Vallette's knights in the Grand Harbour, they first had to capture the garrison at Fort Saint Elmo. For two months under the staggering "lion sun" of June and July, the isolated garrison withstood everything the Turks threw at them. The fort was battered by solid shot, exploding shells, subterranean mines, and repeated human-wave attacks. Finally, when the fort was smashed down to a heap of broken, smoking rubble, the last defender was killed and Barbarossa could turn his siege guns southeast across the Grand Harbour to soften up the Knights' main position.

The inordinate delay, however, had allowed de La Vallette to strengthen his fortifications to the point that the weakened Turkish assault forces—who had suffered unacceptably heavy casualties taking Fort Saint Elmo—were unable to prevail in the main battle for the island. By the onset of rainy autumn, the Turks retreated, leaving half their siege fleet behind them. Malta was solidly in Christian hands. The Knights of Saint John had begun five hundred years before as a medical order dedicated to nursing sick pilgrims to the Holy Land and had been evicted from their possessions successively by superior Muslim forces in a series of sieges: Jerusalem, Cyprus, and Rhodes. Now they had stood their ground, broken the final siege, and beaten the best the Sultan could send against them.

Had they not won this horrible battle, of course, modern history might well have been different. Renaissance Italy, a civilization many historians consider the godmother of modern Europe, probably could not have survived very long if the Turks had taken Malta, then used the island to stage a successful invasion of Sicily and, eventually, the Italian homeland. The Italian states were mercantile powers that depended on maritime commerce for their prosperity. Had Barbarossa controlled the Central Mediterranean from a newly conquered base in Malta, Italy's prosperous commerce would have withered. An impoverished Italy would have been relatively easy prey to a victorious Turkish army. The dominoes, as the saying goes, might have begun to tumble.

But Malta had not fallen. Sulieman the Magnificent had been so physically and spiritually debilitated by the long siege that he died the next year. Jean de La Vallette rebuilt the island's strong points, transforming Malta into the fortress it is today. Six years after the Great Siege, the Knights' fleet took a decisive role in the pivotal naval battle at Lepanto, where the Turks' final attempt to penetrate Western Europe was repulsed.

As I lowered the genoa and furled it along the port rail, I gazed aft at the steep ramparts of the rebuilt Fort Saint Elmo. Thousands of men had murdered each other up there in those terrible, baking days four hundred years ago. Now that we were inside the wings of Sliema harbor, I could feel the stale heat radiating from the limestone. This was October; what had the heat been like in mid-summer? Up on those walls, men in chain mail and steel breastplates had hacked and stabbed their enemies, screaming in the smoky noise, under the domination of the African sun. Every day for months, the madness had continued. Thirst, agony, fear. A slashed limb meant gangrene; capture meant torture and mutilation. The Janizaries had attacked with blaring trumpets, waving scarlet silk banners. The defenders of Saint Elmo had poured burning pitch into their dense ranks. Beneath that lion sun of the Sahara, day after day, for months.

I hitched tight the final sail tie and swung aft to fetch docklines and fenders. Fort Saint Elmo brooded silently above us in the glaring sky.

WITHIN THE PROTECTING ARMS of Malta's creeks were boats of many types, moving in every direction in the deep water. Tourist daytripper boats, jammed with brightly dressed visitors lining the rails and gazing up at the high ramparts of Fort Saint Elmo, skirted around us, rocking us in their wakes. Small open motor launches crisscrossed the many inlets, ferrying passengers from one side to the other like a highway. But mostly, there were yachts; they lined the quay sides and were anchored in every bay and inlet. It looked like the whole of Marsamxett was a marina. We would have to squeeze into a space along the docks, if we could figure out what the local custom was.

Standing on the bow, Doug noticed a uniformed official waving at us. As we had our yellow quarantine flag flying, he would have seen that we were entering Malta for the first time. We followed the instructions the man shouted at us across the expanse of water in a mixture of English and Italian. A few minutes after we had *Matata* securely tied up, in the traditional Mediterranean manner with the anchor laid slightly upwind and two stern warps ashore, two uniformed customs men appeared. A third man, a portly gentleman in a wool suit, although it must have been at least ninety degrees in that brilliant sun, joined these two. All three then proceeded to clamber on board in their heavy leather-soled shoes. Somehow, I didn't feel like requesting them to remove those shoes.

The wool-suited man was the quarantine doctor. He took his job seriously and insisted on going through the whole list of questions, meticulously inscribing each answer on a long form with a fountain pen. The two customs officers poked around in the lockers, an unusual procedure in Mediterranean ports. Normally checking in and out of a country on a yacht is a perfunctory routine, often sweetened with a bottle of Scotch or a few packs of American cigarettes.

"You can lower the yellow flag," Mal called up to Doug, once we had our clearance and our passports had been stamped. But we weren't going to get rid of these fellows so easily. It took another fifteen minutes, during which the obviously senior customs officer continued to ask us questions about our ports of call in Sicily and the junior one wrote down our answers in a notebook, before they seemed satisfied. Malcolm poured them each a half glass of Scotch, which they knocked back in one gulp. The doctor abstained from drinking but did not reject the proferred packs of Marlboros.

"I hope you enjoy Malta," the senior officer said, standing abruptly. He didn't sound like he meant those words, nor did any one of the three smile during the whole grilling. The leader nodded at the two others and they clumped single-file up the steps of the companionway to the cockpit. I noted as I followed them that the hard shoes had scraped the varnish on our steps and engine cover, varnish that had survived months of sun and wet boots but that had never been so ill treated. I rather hoped one of them would land in the water as they jumped ashore from our stern. But alas, we were spared that amusement. The doctor, however, courteously shook Malcolm's hand and gave me a polite dip of his head.

"Whew, what a couple of zombies," I said, flopping onto a cockpit cushion.

Malcolm, too, sat down, exhausted from the long interview. "They couldn't have thought we were smugglers, for God's sake," he said. "That's officialdom at its worst . . . a former colony showing they can run their own show as well as their former masters." Indeed, Malta had only achieved independence from England a relatively short time ago, in 1964.

Now Doug joined us. "What's that smell?" he asked, sniffing the air delicately. I could smell it too, a sour, stinging odor of . . . an outhouse!

Mal looked over the side of the boat at the water swirling around us. "Christ!" he exclaimed, pinching his nose. "That's raw sewage floating there."

Now we all looked, being careful not to breathe in too deeply. Where the wall was broken, a large cement pipe extended out over the lip of the quay and untreated effluent dribbled from it into the water, not ten feet away from our offended noses.

When Mal went ashore to sign us in at the marina office, he requested another slip but was informed that we were lucky we had that one. Then he was told one more bit of bad news. The fee for tying up, *or* anchoring out in the bay, *anywhere* in Malta, was sixty U.S. dollars a month—whether or not you stayed a month or a day, that was the *minimum*. Our planned stay of two nights was going to take a third of the money we had left until we got to Greece. Unless the check was here in Malta, forwarded from the harbor master's office in Gibraltar to the harbor's master here, as we had requested—assuming the check had ever reached Gibraltar—we would be seriously low on cash for the rest of the trip.

The public bus we took to the city gates of Valletta was painted a bright blue and decorated with swirling designs of flowers, both inside and out. Ordinary Maltese people crowded onto the bus at every stop as we rounded the deep inlets of Marsamxett Harbour. An Englishman, the only other non-Maltese, boarded the bus soon after us, and Malcolm went forward to speak to him, to ask directions to the harbor master's office. For good measure, he asked where the main post office was, too, just in case our mail had gone there.

"I live near the post office," the gentleman said. "And I will take you there, but of course we must walk." He continued, "I have just returned from a small holiday."

I noticed the small, worn leather valise at his knee then. He had been in England, he explained as we descended the bus and proceeded through the massive stone gates that lead into the old city of Valletta. A very deep moat, which looked like it could still serve its original function of isolating the city and protecting it, followed the contours of the high walls as far as I could see.

The Englishman had been a planter in another former British colony, Kenya. Like many of his compatriots, he had found England dreary and too expensive to settle in after his land had been taken away and he was forced to retire. He had chosen to seek a haven in Malta, but it could just as easily have been Gibraltar, Tangier, or Mallorca. "But now it is becoming very difficult," our friend confided. "Since we were forced to close our naval facility, the economy has declined." Libya, he explained, had recently begun to fill that economic gap, selling oil cheaply to Malta and providing her with loans. The newly elected socialist government had no qualms about dealing with Qaddafi. "One sees many Libyans here now . . . entertaining themselves." The gentleman's bristly mustache twitched with emotion.

"The Beirut of the Maghreb," Malcolm suggested, a place for

Arabs to retreat to, away from their own country's strict Muslim prohibitions on alcohol and high living.

Our kind escort lead us through the steep streets of Valletta, along narrow caverns overshadowed by huge, ornate stone buildings, a legacy of the Knights of Saint John. The narrowness of the streets almost precluded any motorized vehicle traffic. The side streets often were stepped besides. But there were pushcarts and cleverly contrived devices for lifting loads up and down long stone stairways.

At the post office we said goodbye to our friend. "I'm sorry that I cannot invite you for a spot of something, but there is no electricity again and the house is unbearable without the fan." Private homes were only allowed to use electric power a few hours a day, he informed us. As we watched him trudging up the street with his small grip, I noted how his shoulders slumped now. The retirement that he must have looked forward to and expected to enjoy in this previously British enclave had turned sour for him.

A chilly desk clerk flipped through the *M*s in the *poste restante* mail box. "There is nothing for McConnell or . . . *Matata*," he said, turning his back to us.

"But there must be . . . " I cried.

Malcolm took my elbow and firmly turned me toward the door. "It's okay, we'll try the harbor master's office, where the ships dock in Grand Harbour."

After being sent from one run-down office to another near the docks, we finally reached a dead end. "This is not for yachts," the last clerk said. He was about thirty, with the fine-boned, small-featured, and darkly handsome face of many Maltese. Looking at his fingers drumming on a pile of papers impatiently, I suddenly realized that his self-important attitude was reminiscent of another that I knew quite well: that of the minor Greek bureaucrat. As I had seen so often in Rhodes, at the bank or in some government office where I'd gone to get a form or document prepared, this man sported one long fingernail on the little finger of his right hand. It was nearly an inch and curved like a talon. This affectation is popular among a class of men who do not want to be mistaken for common laborers: they had risen above working with their hands.

"Let's go, Honey," Malcolm said quietly. Malcolm's tone of voice belied the fury I saw he was trying to conceal. I tended to get angry and argue with functionaries; Mal was a much more practiced diplomat and knew that it was the superior to whom he should voice his complaint. Before we left Malta, I thought, some official was going to hear just what Malcolm thought of the treatment we had received as visitors.

Our walking tour of Valletta, as interested as we were in the history of this stronghold of the Knights of Saint John—the same Knights who had been in Rhodes until they were defeated and banished, to settle here—was tainted by the unpleasant manners and rudeness of the officials we dealt with. The ordinary Maltese people were polite toward us tourists, however, as if politeness was natural to them. We wondered if there was some sort of official edict to treat strangers as interlopers that the bureaucrats were carrying out. This attitude was in contrast to the government's stated desire to increase the tourist trade of Malta.

On our return to the marina, we decided to try the office once more in case some mail had arrived during the day. There *was* a letter addressed to S/Y *Matata*, but it wasn't for us. Curious, we asked if there was another yacht named *Matata* registered at the marina.

We found them moored not far from us. The other *Matata* was a forty-foot yawl flying a blue British ensign from her stern. The owner was retired Royal Air Force. He and his wife welcomed us on board when we explained that we, too, had named our boat *Matata*. John and Susan had retired to Kenya, where he had managed an aircraft maintenance plant until recently. They were now fulfilling a lifelong dream of living aboard their own boat and sailing where and when they wanted.

Mal asked how they had come to name their boat *Matata*. John explained that they had learned Swahili while living in East

Africa, as we had when we worked in the U.S. Embassy in Leopoldville and later in Kigali, Rwanda. One of the words used familiarly and almost unconsciously, was *matata*, meaning variously an argument, trouble, or war, depending on the context.

"Boats are always trouble," John pointed out, "as much as you may love them, there's always a problem."

Our boat got its name in a more roundabout fashion. As Malcolm started to explain, I noticed a book prominently displayed on the shelves against the forward bulkhead. *Matata* was the title; the author: Malcolm McConnell. I pointed at it. "That's how *Matata* got her name. Mal wrote that novel about the war in the Congo in the sixties and when we bought the boat it seemed a fitting name for her. You see, she's really named after a book, which was originally named for the experience."

Susan reached for the book and opened it for Mal to sign. "See," she said indicating the blank first page, "it was a gift from friends who knew we named *our* boat *Matata.*"

Malcolm inscribed his name beneath the original giver's. John whisked away our tea cups and poured us tumblers of Scotch to toast the two *Matata*s.

Whenever we are in a country or region new to me, I read the local newspaper and I like to browse in a typical bookstore. In particular, I always buy a cookbook that includes native food recipes. Even though we were low on cash, we now decided that there was enough money to dine out ashore one more time, buy a cookbook for me and a history of Malta for Malcolm, and still have sufficient cash until we reached Greece, where the check would either have arrived or we could borrow from one of our friends in Lindos until it did. This decision, once made, was like having a depressing fog melt around us. Malta seemed a much brighter place to visit. And I was especially pleased to add a very unusual cookbook to my collection.

The food people eat and the manner in which it is prepared is not only an indication of what is available locally (in this case a plethora of rabbit and fish) but points out the cultural influences and biases of the region. For instance, I considered Lampuki Pie first kin to English steak and kidney pie. Since fish, particularly lampuki (dolphin fish), was regularly caught in the strait nearby, the Maltese had simply adapted the typical "pie" method of English cookery using this basic ingredient. With the addition of pitted black olives and chopped tomatoes, a taste of Italy was thrown in.

As pleased as I was to have the cookbook, I wanted to sample a typical Maltese meal. That evening, we—Doug too, although he was apprehensive as to what sort of culinary treat he was in store for this time—boarded a bus for the town of Sliema, the largest city on the mainland. I had seen a typical Maltese restaurant advertised in the local newspaper and was determined to find it. With the aid of a map from the tourist bureau, we walked from the bus in search of the "Capricorn."

In contrast to walled Valletta, we now found ourselves traversing wide boulevards bordered by graciously proportioned two- and three-story stone villas. I couldn't resist peeking into lighted windows and vestibules and was amazed at the opulence displayed in these eighteenth- and early nineteenth-century grand houses. But, as Malcolm pointed out, even these residents had limited electricity and water.

The restaurant was situated in one of these houses. It was obviously a family-run affair, and popular with Maltese, as almost every table was filled. We were the only tourists in this out-of-the-way place.

After reading about one of the favorite outings for Maltese families—a fried rabbit picnic—I elected to try rabbit. Malcolm chose octopus stew. Lucky for Doug, there were a few more familiar dishes on the short menu; he enjoyed a steak and showed no interest in sampling our fare.

The water shortage was apparent next day when I turned the tap on at the dock and discovered there wasn't a drop. "You're in luck," the elderly, grizzled man on the boat next to us said. "We get to use the water point for one hour, one day a week, and this afternoon is it." I looked at his boat with new respect. It was nearly spotless; the white fiber glass hull shone with a recent shining and the varnished doghouse glowed brightly. We decided to postpone our departure a few hours until after we had the use of the water hose to top off our tanks.

"I discovered a really good pub," Doug said, using the word "pub" almost naturally. "All the crews hang out there."

At his suggestion, we escaped from the sewer stench surrounding *Matata* and walked around the bay to the pub. There was Willy whom we'd met in Ibiza, at the bar, drinking a mug of bitter and nodding enthusiastically at what his companion was saying. Soon, we all had mugs and Willy ordered a round of bacon and fried-egg sandwiches. The tall blond man was telling his audience what it had been like last month racing in the ill-fated Fastnet Race in England.

"We were well ahead and missed the worst of the gale," he said, shaking his head. "I'll tell you, those people shouldn't be allowed to go out in those small boats in that kind of weather . . . " By small, he meant our size.

We sailed late that afternoon, our course set for Crete, 600 miles away. The blond man's words echoed in my head long after Malta had dropped over the horizon. But I had faith in our small boat, and in Malcolm and Doug, and in myself. There was risk, certainly, but again I felt confident that our preparations and skill were equal to whatever the sea and the weather ahead could throw at us.

CHAPTER NINE

OCTOBER 20, 1145
MERIDIAN PASS OF THE SUN: 35° 41' NORTH
17° 55' EAST

The wind blew north-northeast, a solid weight of 40 knots. Every few minutes, gusts over 50 knots slammed the double-reefed mainsail and storm jib, and fist-sized balls of spray pounded on the highside coachroof. The sun was bright at midday, but the chill northerly had washed all the heat from the sky. The sea was running steep and wild; cold, glittery blue, seemingly a winter ocean. Malta and the stagnant Sahara sun were three days behind us.

I was bundled in a full set of oilskins, my thick blue seaboots, foam flotation vest, and safety harness. Kneeling as best I could on the high, portside cockpit bench, I tried to shield the sextant from the worst of the spray. Behind me, the blade of the wind vane slapped and tottered in the cold gale. Double shock cords reinforced the weather-side tiller lines. *Matata* swooped and staggered, taking the wind and swell on the port beam, clanking east under storm sails at almost 6 knots.

Using my teeth, I peeled back the tightly snapped yellow cuff of my oilskin sleeve and peered at my watch. It was 1144 and twenty seconds. Time to start measuring the meridian pass.

"Okay, Carol," I yelled above the wind and the groans of the fiber glass hull.

Carol slid back the main hatch about two inches and showed her face above the storm boards. Despite the angle of heel and the violent snap-rolls as we rose to meet each steep swell, she appeared calm, rested but alert. We'd been in this wind for over twenty-four hours. Our dead reckoning gave us an estimated daily run of ninety-eight miles, not bad for storm sails. Once I got the sun's meridian altitude, I could plot a noon fix and correct the DR.

I steadied my right boot sole on the lowside cockpit coaming and wrapped my left arm around the weather sheet winch, so that I was free to grasp the sextant handle in my right hand and twirl the micrometer drum with my left thumb and forefinger. Getting an accurate sight with this amount of sea running was not going to be easy, but I'd grown accustomed to the problem out on the Atlantic.

"How's it look?" Carol called. "Are you getting any kind of a horizon?"

I adjusted the sextant's index arm to 50 degrees elevation, raised the instrument to my eye and prepared to scan the rolling horizon to the south. Even with one arm around the winch and my feet braced on the lowside, I felt clumsy and unstable. After readjusting my weight, I tried again. This time I flew halfway across the steeply heeled cockpit and slumped into a heap in the spray-soaked well, almost smacking the sextant on the engine gear arm in the process.

Again I wedged myself on the highside bench, and again a steep swell struck the boat and tossed me from my perch. I knew that it was 1145 and the pass had begun. If I didn't catch the sun at its zenith, I wouldn't get an accurate local noon latitude.

"Open the hatch all the way," I shouted, pulling myself reasonably upright and trying as I did to untangle the lines of the safety harness and also shelter the sextant.

Carol slammed open the companionway hatch as I lurched against the storm boards. Instinctively, she grabbed the wet webbing of my harness. She was crouched on her own unstable perch atop the engine box, but she was able to clutch the overhead grab rail with her right hand and steady me with her left. Doug swung out of the main cabin, using the grab rails like an orangutan. Carol spoke to him, but her words were lost in the wind. I knew, though, that she had told Doug to note the times and sextant elevations on the navigation log she had already prepared.

Once more I raised the sextant and jammed the rubber eyepiece against my face. The cool, brassy mirror image of the sun's disc hung out there in space, just above the dancing angles of the horizon. I breathed deeply, then exhaled. The sound of the wind seemed to drop away; the motion of the boat seemed to ease. I lost awareness of everything except the sun's image and the blue line of the southern horizon. This unconscious focusing while taking a sight was not a trick I'd learned from John Calvert or any other old salt. It was a mindless Zen maneuver that I had slowly acquired on the Atlantic. All those days of cold northerlies en route to the Azores, I performed this same transcendental exercise. I literally forgot about the sextant; I disregarded the noise of the gale, the violent motion of the boat. I forced myself to believe that there was a geometrically perfect horizon off to the south, a flat Euclydian intersection *waiting* to be kissed and stroked by the ripe curve of the sun's lower limb. I was not a sailor, carrying out a difficult feat of navigation. I was, instead, a privileged witness to an exhibition of pure, universal mathematics.

"Mark," I intoned. "HS forty-nine fifty-one."

"Eleven hours," Carol chanted back like some Druid priestess, "forty-five minutes and . . . twenty-six seconds."

Again, I held the sun's disc on the seemingly flat horizon, only partially conscious that my left thumb and forefinger were caressing the fine-adjustment knob of the micrometer drum, raising the metallic lower limb a few minutes of arc. "Mark," I called again. The sun stood still on the hard blue horizon. This was the meridian pass. I shouted the sextant height, and Carol repeated the liturgy of the time.

"That's it," I said, twisting out of her grasp to flop down on the lowside bench.

Now the reality of the bright, windy day and the clattering boat returned. The swells marched drunkenly down from the north and I felt the torque and staggering heel. I was back from the abstract world of navigation.

When Carol had worked up the sight and plotted our position, she pulled open the top storm boards and tottered into the cockpit. I helped her snap her safety harness clip to a highside stanchion. She looked pale and queasy. "Not so veddy, veddy pleasant down there," she managed in a mock-Edwardian voice. Closing her eyes, she inhaled deeply several times, then leaned back on the cushions to survey the wild seascape. "If I hadn't just looked at the calendar," she said, her voice calm again, her breathing even, "I'd say this was a meltemi and we were reaching from Mykonos to Ikaria."

"More like a bora in the Adriatic," I replied, and pointed east. "See that cloud bank out there?"

She nodded without looking up. "I saw it when you were taking the sight. What do you think?"

"Big damn sirocco blowing in Greece. Two, maybe three hundred miles from here." I looked around the cloudless blue sky above us. "At least it's a fair wind. The first really good one we've had since leaving Gib."

Now Carol rose and braced herself on the sheet winch. She thrust her face squarely into the weight of the wind, mindless of the occasional spray. "It's wonderful," she said, her eyes closed, her body moving easily with the snap and roll of the boat. "We logged more than a hundred miles since yesterday. At this rate, we'll be in Crete in two days."

"Greece," I muttered, the word springing unbidden from my thoughts. "*Greece.* Jesus, for a while there, I didn't think we'd actually make it." I scanned the tightly reefed, salt-blasted sails and the rigid telltales. Around us, the sea was heaped with slashing blue swell-faces and long, foamy crests. I could actually *feel* our relentless progress east. "I don't know why," I called above the chill wind, "but somehow, today . . . *now,* I know we'll make it."

Carol sank back into the shelter of her oilskins, smiling, her eyes closed again against the reflected sunglare. She was an American woman in her late thirties, fully at peace with herself and the six-ton conglomerate of plastics and metal that carried her across the wild sea toward the ancient nation to the east.

At sunset, the wind rose to over 50 knots and began to overpower the boat. Doug had the watch, and I was trying to sleep in the starboard quarterberth while Carol rested in the lowside bunk in the main cabin. We both were jolted from our dozing rest when the boat took an especially hard gust and swung hard up on the wind. I was still in my oilskins, and I managed to drag myself to the cockpit in one clumsy but reasonably quick motion.

Doug was crouched against the spray at the tiller, dragging the bow back down off the wind. To the east, the sky was now covered with a distant line of pulsing thunderheads that were gilded with silvery detail by the last of the sun.

"Got some pretty bad puffs there," Doug said with tight-lipped but reasonably convincing bravado.

The sea was a field of cold blue pyramids and spray. I snapped up my safety harness clip and pulled myself to the highside to study the wind and sea. The boat was still riding all right, but the vane would never accept this amount of weather helm. It was time to drop the main completely and ride out the blow on the storm jib.

I slumped back down to the shelter of the coachroof. *Shit,* I thought bitterly, *why does it always happen when it's getting dark?*

As if reading my mind, Carol threw back the hatch and dumped herself into the cockpit, dressed in full oilskins, sea boots, and safety harness.

"Gotta drop the main," I called. "Carol, take the tiller. Doug, you handle the sheet." I turned my face into the wind, then flinched back from the spray. "We can't head up to drop it, not with this goddamn sea. So . . . just ease the sheet when I let the halyard go."

I snatched some sodden elastic sail stops from the cockpit cubby, adjusted the briny plates of my oilskins beneath the web of safety harness, and hauled myself up to the port rail. Moving along the highside deck was not as hard as I had feared. Carol knew the boat perfectly and could steer well in this wind. But I still had to plot and scheme each lurching step and handhold. My safety harness clip dragged along behind me, snagging every few feet where the jackline was fouled. Finally, in a mixture of frustration and fear, I unclipped the line and snapped the caribiner to the forward shroud. Stumbling around the wet, jolting deck, my oilskin hood had jammed down the knit wool watch cap I wore beneath it. I was half-blinded, steamy with sweat under the weight of the jacket, vest, and harness. In the time since I'd come on deck, the gusts had strengthened considerably. Carol was now having difficulty keeping the boat on a reach.

"Ease the damn main," I yelled at Doug, venting my own anxiety and anger.

Doug slacked a foot on the mainsheet, and we seemed to ride a little better. I was hanging on the port shrouds like a groggy boxer on the ropes. When I relinquished my hold on the taut cables of the rigging, gravity would hurl me down against the mast. Unfortunately, the main halyard winch was on the low, starboard side. In order to drop the sail, I'd have to swing around to the other side, cling to the slick, wet alloy of the mast with one hand to keep from being thrown overboard, tighten the topping lift the proper amount, then uncleat the coiled halyard with my free fingers. If all went well, the sail would be down in a matter of seconds, but if the salty halyard coil snarled, we'd have a nasty problem, the sail slack in the gale, flogging itself to pieces.

I stalled, indecisive, suddenly quite afraid of the dark gale howling past my face. Beneath my feet, the boat twisted and dropped, pounded in the trough, then staggered up the next swell-face. I made my move.

As I had feared, my boot soles slipped on the wet deck, and I was thrown violently against the cold alloy mast, smacking my right cheekbone painfully as I hit. I jammed my right hand between the taut sail luff and the mast track and clawed for some kind of hold. With my uncoordinated left hand I flailed away at the coiled halyard until it was running free.

"Okay, Doug," I called. "Ease her. Slow . . . "

Doug was crouched in the cockpit, below the mainsheet traveler on the coachroof. As he eased out the line, we were struck by an exceptionally violent gust. A heavy, crashing wave washed across the cabintop. Doug had not been wearing a safety harness when he took the watch and he had not put one on after he came on deck. He seized a handrail in one hand and tried to hold the sheet in the other. I was dragging down the sail with both hands, my back jammed against the slack lee rigging when the boom flew out to strike my belly and the thick fabric of the mainsail flailed in my face. My first impulse was anger, at Doug's apparent incompetence and Carol's sloppy steering. Then I heard Carol scream something, shrill and indistinct. When I had most of the billowing sail down and bunched between my two arms against the yawing boom, I could see aft.

Doug was halfway out of the boat, his right leg actually over the rail, in the water. He looked like he'd been hit by a pressure hose at some violent street demonstration. His hat was gone, his hair streamed with cold seawater. There was a flat deadness to his eyes. Behind him, Carol looked pale with shock. Doug recovered in a moment and yanked the mainsheet in to dampen the wildly swinging boom. Braced now on the steady boom, I could swing aft to furl and lash down the sail.

We rode much easier without the main, but we were still moving fast on this beam reach, the scrap of a storm jib hauling us along at 4 knots. I squared away the loose tackle at the mast and worked my way back to the highside to retrace my route to the cockpit. By the time I got there, Carol and Doug had reset the wind vane and were coiling down sheets. No one spoke. We were all still stunned by the near-disaster. Obviously, if Doug had been thrown overboard with this wind and this sea running, weighted down by sodden oilskins, with the cold darkness thick around the boat. . . . There was no need for us to speak of the incident. Doug was crouched again beneath the shelter of the coachroof, shivering with cold and runaway emotions.

"I'll take the watch for a while," I said, patting him on the wet shoulder in a hollow, unconvincing gesture of camaraderie. "Go down and get some dry clothes on."

"I'm okay," Doug answered. He wiped his hand across his dripping mustache and pulled his jacket hood over his head. Without looking directly at the hard ranks of swells that rolled down at us from the north, he nodded vaguely windward. "That was some damn wave that hit us. We almost . . . "

His voice trailed away. There was nothing to be gained from speaking.

I nodded in the windy darkness. Doug stared at the cuffs of his oilskin trousers, his expression loose, his eyes now showing the painful recognition that his young life had almost ended a few minutes earlier out in that rolling black sea.

There were stars, a lopsided chunk of moon, and the cold black wind. Reaching east under storm jib, the motion was not too violent, but we all felt better eating in the cockpit than down in the closed cabin where the inevitable odor of the bilge mixed with the stale oil and diesel fumes. We hunched over our deep soup bowls and spooned the hot canned stew that Carol had gamely prepared down at the swaying galley stove. She'd mixed a large can of Italian minestrone with a smaller can of Heinz chicken and dumplings we'd bought in Gib. After some imaginative spicing, the concoction was quite pleasant.

I had opened one of our last good bottles of decent wine to alleviate the gloomy atmosphere. It was too rough for glasses or even plastic mugs, so the three of us passed the bottle among us in the cockpit while the stew warmed us. We talked about Greece, about Lindos and the people Doug would meet there. We did not discuss the wind.

After we'd sopped up the last of the stew with a few remaining heels of Maltese bread, we read the log, scanned the crazy horizon for shipping, and set the watch rotation. I would take the helm until 2200, Doug until midnight, and Carol would wake me at 0200. Carol went below and was braced against the chart table, making a plausible attempt to wipe down the galley sink, when a gray blur fluttered past my face and tumbled through the companionway, into the brightly lit cabin.

Carol yelled, a squeak of unreasoning alarm. Then she laughed. Doug and I almost bumped heads as we lunged toward the open hatch. A lovely yellow and black warbler was perched squarely on the peak of her woolen cap. Like the bird we'd rescued near Sardinia, this little fellow was utterly spent, so exhausted that he was incapable of further flight, or of showing the slightest fear of humans. We climbed down to crowd around Carol as she stood stiffly conscious of the weight on her cap.

The bird's eyes were like shiny brown pellets, liquid in his soft yellow face. His small claws were locked into the knit wool. When Carol swayed with the boat's roll, the bird swayed in unison.

"I guess I'll have to stand here all night," she said.

Doug stepped closer. "I'll take him," he whispered.

Slowly raising his open hand, Doug scooped the bird delicately off Carol's cap and turned, moving with controlled speed so as not to alarm the bird. The book rack above the chart table provided a logical perch for our new passenger. He clamped his little talons to the varnished restraining bar, glanced once about the cabin, then lowered his bright head to sleep.

Carol went to her bunk in the main cabin and Doug pulled off his oilskins in preparation for sleep. I closed the hatch and settled down in the glow of the compass lamp to face the two empty hours of my watch. Ten minutes later, however, I saw that there was still a light burning down below and quietly slipped open the hatch to make sure Doug hadn't fallen asleep with the chart table light still on.

Doug was not asleep. He sat comfortably at the head of the quarter-berth, his elbows on the chart table, gazing up at the little bird that swayed slowly in his sleep. There was something in Doug's expression of calm satisfaction that showed me I should not interrupt this scene by speaking. Taking both sides of the hatch in my hands, I slid the briney fiber glass softly closed. When I sat down again near the tiller, I recognized the emotion I had seen in Doug's eyes. Kinship, connection. . . . He was empathizing with that small being who had almost died in the dark gale.

MALCOLM WAS PERCHED on the cabintop, peering through the binoculars. For the past two hours we had been expecting to see land—the island of Kithera or her southern sister, Anti-Kithera. these two islands effectively made a bridge between the Peloponnese of Greece and the western tip of Crete, broken only by three rock-strewn channels. As our intention was to skirt the northern coast of Crete on our passage eastward toward the bottom of Rhodes Island, we wanted to pass through the southern channel, that between Anti-Kithera and the westernmost cape of Crete.

After these past four wild sailing days and yesterday's difficulty getting a sun sight with the heavy overcast, we were not absolutely certain how far north we were. But we hoped to get a confirmation of our position in the next two hours before dark. Otherwise, we would have to follow the prudent course and head south to avoid running into those sparsely lighted islands that lay ahead of us.

"I got it." The relief in Mal's voice was apparent. "Here, I'll take the helm," he said, handing me the glasses. "You're eyes are better than mine." I relinquished the tiller and followed his pointing finger. There was indeed a distant, darker gray out in that gray ocean. But which piece of land was it?

I had read Denham's guide to sailing in these waters just this afternoon, and he had dramatically pointed out that the channel between the Peloponnese and Kithera was littered with wrecks, and the middle channel between the sister islands had menaced more than one ship over the centuries. We would have to get a lot closer to that gray shadow though, before I could tell exactly where we were.

Matata charged ahead at 5 knots, under power. The wind had dropped this morning, but the sky was still overcast and visibility was deteriorating. So far it wasn't raining. "I just hope we can pick up a light before this weather closes in," I said, as much to Malcolm as myself. I hated this awkward time before dusk with land close by and no exact reference points.

"We will, we will," he answered, but he leaned forward and increased the throttle slightly to gain another knot.

An hour passed and we were six miles closer to that gray blob.

A smaller, satellite rock appeared now off a tall cape. North of the main mass we could see a clear expanse of sea opening up. I brought the chart up on deck again and we checked and rechecked our bearings until we were sure. That was Kithera. We would have Anti-Kithera on our starboard bow soon.

"I got it," Mal said in a tired monotone. "Okay, let's set our course for south of Anti-Kithera.

"Right." I went below again and worked out our new course, marking the direction with a light pencil line from our dead-reckoning position to the center of the channel. We should pick up the light on the southern end of Anti-Kithera in two hours, well after full dark. My eyes swam with tiredness, but I knew Mal had been on watch for over two hours now and I should relieve him. Doug was sleeping soundly, and he'd need to be rested for the approach to the channel as well.

"Tired?" Mal asked as I joined him in the cockpit.

"Kind of," I admitted. I ached all over, in fact, from the severe knocking around we'd taken for days, compounded by a lack of sleep. I slid along the cockpit seat into Malcolm's curving arm and we rested there a long time without talking. But my head nodded; my eyes were too heavy to keep open.

"You go down and get a little sleep. I'll call you as soon as I get the light." Mal smiled reassuringly at me and gave me a little shove toward the companionway. "Carol," he said, before I stepped down, "just measure the distance from the channel to Hania. I think we'll check into Greece there instead of going all the way to Heraklion, okay? We're all too tired."

"Great idea." As I bent over the chart table I felt mixed emotions: relief that by noon tomorrow we would be in another safe harbor for a day of rest, but also apprehensive. Here we were, making a night approach again on an unknown channel that would be busy with shipping. But I climbed into my bunk and concentrated on getting to sleep. I had to be prepared for my watch in a couple of hours, rested and alert.

Doug was shaking me. "What's wrong?" I asked, struggling out of my sleeping bag.

"Nothing, you were really asleep." Doug grinned down at me in the dimly lit cabin. "We've got the light on the channel and Mal wants you up there."

"Already?" I fumbled to see my watch. I had been asleep for three hours; it was already 10:00 P.M. Mal would be very tired. Groggily, I dressed in my damp oilskins. Mal and Doug were both in the cockpit, Doug on the helm. "Two or three mugs of coffee? I called above the sound of the engine.

"Make it two," Mal answered. "I'm going to get some sleep and you sit up here with Doug, okay? At least until we get through the channel." I could barely see his face in the pinkish glow from the compass light, but even from several feet away, I could tell he was shivering. When I climbed up on deck with the hot coffee, I understood why. There was a fine mist falling and the temperature had dropped markedly. It was going to be a rotten night.

It took us three hours to transit the channel. Doug steered while I dozed on the cockpit bench, periodically reviving myself to help him identify and sort out a ship's lights or to peer into the dark night and try to distinguish the black shapes of rocks on either side of the channel. At dawn, as Doug slept in the cockpit and I steered, we had the second of Crete's high, rugged capes off our starboard beam. The rain had stopped, but I was so stiff and weary it hardly mattered. I woke Doug to write up the log at the change of watch. It was time to call Malcolm to take over.

But I didn't have to call him. A cheerful, rested Malcolm appeared in the galley and waved up at me. He and Doug were talking down there, but I couldn't hear them over the engine noise.

"Mal said," Doug repeated, leaning into the cockpit, "how about some bacon and eggs? He's cooking."

Suddenly the night was gone, the grayness of the sea around me took on a slight bluish cast, the aquamarine of the Aegean. "Hey, yes," I called back. "I'm starved." Already I could smell the aroma of fresh coffee rising from the galley. They must have made real filter coffee, I realized, not the same old instant. "Mal,"

I called again. "I'll have my eggs sunny side up."

He waved up at me and I could see that he, too, was feeling good about the day. In a few hours we would officially be back in Greece.

CHAPTER TEN

OCTOBER 27, AFTERNOON
HANIA, CRETE

I sat in the comfortable leather sling-chair, my wet deck shoes propped on the marble hearth, letting the heat of the fire dry my socks. The café was meso-sixties, pseudo-jetset—whitewashed stone walls, woven tapestries, a good collection of nineteenth-century nautical brass artfully hung here and there. The tables were well separated and, for Greece, the overhead lighting was an absolute model of restraint. A stereo played vintage Judy Collins.

Doug came back from the bar with two fresh Metaxa brandies. Our wet oilskin jackets were spread on the third chair; a chess set was open on the low oak table before us. Rain rattled and clicked on the steamy window facing the harbor. Fifty yards down the old stone quay *Matata* was moored alongside, well snugged down with spring lines to dampen the roll of the reflected swell that worked its way around the sea wall and into this old Venetian harbor. For the past eighteen hours, a force eight sirocco had been blowing across the southern Aegean. Here, on the western cape of Crete, the wind had been almost due east, channeled along the northern coast of the long island by the steep, unbroken ridge of Levka Ori, the White Mountains. We were once more stormbound by the violence of the Middle Sea's autumn weather.

I took the glass from Doug and sipped, studying the pattern of the chessmen on the board. Judy Collins was now singing sweetly about clouds and love and seeing life from both sides. Squinting in the orange flare of the cedar logs, warm in my dry jeans and thick wool turtleneck, it was easy to forget the weather and that we still had almost three hundred miles to sail before reaching Lindos. At the tables around us, groups of young foreigners sat hunched over wine bottles and *tavli* boards, their conversations a murmur of Dutch, Midlands English, and Swedish. Doug did not seem inclined to hurry his move, so I slid deeper in my chair and let myself indulge in a few minutes of sixties' nostalgia.

The kids at the other tables certainly abetted my reverie. They were long-haired and sported a couple of shaggy beards. One boy wore a braided leather headband to hold back his lank blond hair; another was draped in a thick Andean poncho of soft striped wool. The girls all wore maxies or Afghan coats. An inevitable rank of aluminum-frame backpacks stood beside each group's table.

I was a little punchy from cumulative lack of sleep, but, if I squinted more, I felt a definite rush of time-machine *déjà vu*. This was not Crete in 1979 but Costa's bar in Lindos, circa 1969. That tall, stoop-shouldered blond boy was Henrik, the depressive poet from Copenhagen; that slight girl with the wavy red hair was Tiger, the psychedelic painter from Melbourne. The stereo tape played on. Now Procol Harum chanted an electronic dirge about a whiter shade of pale. At the surrounding tables, these European kids in their early twenties swayed and nodded to the beat of music that had been popular when they were small children.

Doug saw me watching our neighbors. "Are there a lot of places like this in Greece?"

He meant the people, not the café itself. It was a good question.

I hadn't been in Crete for years, but in Rhodes, I knew, high prices and middle-class package tourism had driven away backpackers five years earlier. The expansive prosperity of the 1960s had also evaporated in almost every European country except West Germany. The counter-culture was no longer as *convenient* as it once was, and the once-ubiquitous "student" generation that migrated annually from Amsterdam to Katmandu had been reduced to a thin band of stragglers. And most of the kids in this café were far removed from the Peace-and-Love naiveté of their predecessors. They didn't look much like students, despite the masquerade accuracy of their clothes and hair.

My guess was that they belonged to that sad new class of unemployed school leavers, failed apprentices, and other rootless working-class outcasts that swell the ranks of the various squatter armies that had recently appeared in almost every large European city. These particular kids had acquired the coloration of a more prosperous older generation. Some of their peers chose the Day Glo Mohawks and plumage of the No Future Punks. Others I'd seen in Milan, Paris, and even Madrid had adopted quite convincing Hell's Angels disguises. What these young people had in common was the dreary recognition that they had fallen through the gaping cracks now ripping through the fabric of West European industrial society.

They were untrained for the high-technology trades in which the only promise of work could be found. Most weren't prepared either academically or by virtue of class tradition to make the quantum jump to the professions by entering university, and, even if they had been, the inflexible academic-vocational track divergence of the European education systems had damned them forever, at age fifteen, to the working classes. Unlike Willy and Gordon, and the couple I'd met in Gib aboard *Sarga*, these young people didn't seem to have the resourcefulness to blast out of their unfairly imposed status.

Instead of finding steady work in some unconventional field, they drifted, picking up a few hundred francs here, a few thousand lire there, working the wine harvests with Algerian migrants and passing the cold months in kibbutz factories in the Negev. Often, they fantasized about emigrating to Australia or Canada. They weren't looking for enlightenment or universal brotherhood on the road. Their needs were more modest: cheap food, cheap alcohol, and a cheap place to sleep, preferably in a warm climate. They pooled their meager resources by necessity, not out of any romantic notion of transcultural Woodstock fraternity. And, I knew, when conditions got bad or an easy opportunity arose, they stole from their traveling companions or local merchants with little inhibition.

I imagined this contingent of young travelers was en route south and east, toward Israel, where they could winter in the sunshine, picking kibbutz citrus fruit and, on weekends, smoking hash on the broad white beach at Elat. The early harsh weather had driven them south, to take temporary refuge in Greece before the deck-class ferryboat passage to Haifa. In many ways, they were just as pathetic as that little yellow bird who had been blown away from his migrating flock and had sought refuge in our boat.

I sipped my brandy, letting the log fire toast my damp toes. A month earlier in Ibiza, we had witnessed one manifestation of Europe's roller-coaster economy. Young German computer programmers and technocrats flaunted their wealth and greedy hedonism as they boogied in their lavender flight suits under the strobes and pulsing laser beams. Ironically, despite the claims of European unity under the Common Market, young Germans were still sampling the fruits of incredible economic prosperity. No common thread of unity connected those young Germans in Ibiza to these unemployed Europeans whose countries' economic fortunes had faltered. The Dutch and Belgian kids huddled around the tables of this quiet, tasteful café, nursing fifty-drachma bottles of Marko retsina, represented the other side of the story. The welfare states they came from gave them enough to survive on the various over-burdened dole systems, but, as the punk-rockers loved to remind adult society, this entire class of young people really did not have a future.

I knocked back the Metaxa and rose automatically to get a refill. Outside the wind pounded through the narrow harbor, sending up sheets of spray from the cobblestones along the quay. Carol was on board the boat, using the privacy to wash her hair and indulge in the luxury of a hot, fresh-water sponge bath. We hoped to sail in the morning; today was a respite, a limbo day imposed by nature. Yesterday, despite a low overcast, falling barometer, and all the signs of an impending blow, we had left Hania, en route for Rhodes. But, as soon as we cleared the mouth of the crumbling Venetian sea wall, the state of the sea and wind outside the sheltered harbor became evident. The swell swept into the wide arms of Hania Bay, high from the east-northeast. At the tip of the eastern cape the sea was running over fifteen feet, that close, pyramid sea that made beating such a nightmare. Naturally, when we finally rounded the cape in a horizontal downpour, the main axis of the gale was right on our rhumb line, 85 degrees magnetic. Reluctantly, we turned back for the snug shelter of Hania's medieval harbor.

Our temporary setback hadn't been entirely unfortunate, however. That afternoon, in this café, we'd met our present benefactor, a young American backpacker named Barry. He'd been on the road for years, but, unlike his European counterparts, Barry had a lucrative profession. He was a skilled stonemason and had just come off a ten-month stint reconstructing a farm house in the Midi for a well-known British actor. In short, Barry had money, and he was lonely for the company of other Americans.

When he saw *Matata*'s American ensign fluttering wetly at pier-side, he called down to the boat. We were in the café, spending the very last of our cash on sandwiches and Fix beer. I called to Barry from the café doorway and he came ambling in, a warm smile on his face, to pump our hands with his hydraulic press of a grip. Barry was a big teddy bear of a guy in French worker's blue overalls, tall and broad with an easy smile and strangely mobile eyes.

By the time Barry had paid for a bottle of Metaxa and several rounds of beers to chase the brandy with, we were all fast friends. With typical American generosity, Barry dug into his embroidered Turkish wallet and extracted a handful of twenty-dollar bills. "Hey," he said, thrusting the money at me, "I'll bum a ride on your boat to Lindos, and you can pay me back there."

I hesitated. Opposite me at the table, I saw Carol's expression of ambivalence. We needed cash badly, but she was very hesitant about accepting a loan from this young stranger. It had not been formally decided that we'd carry him with us to Lindos, and, if I took the money, I'd be tacitly agreeing to this condition. But our food stock on board was reduced to some rusty canned goods and damp pasta. We needed fresh produce, we needed canned juice, milk, margarine, the lot. We also needed twenty gallons of diesel fuel, and that alone would cost almost fifty dollars.

I reached out and took the stiff sheaf of new American bills. "Okay, Barry," I said, shaking his muscular hand, "you've got a deal."

That night we climbed up the cobbled road from the harbor and indulged ourselves in a taverna meal of mousaka, pastichio, roast lamb, fried okra, zucchini, and eggplant, all washed down by multiple bottles of good Demestica red. We were definitely back in Greece, and we suddenly had enough money to enjoy ourselves.

Barry came bursting through the café's arched doorway, bringing with him a waft of damp air. He pulled off his dripping rubber poncho and stood, back to the fire to warm his legs.

"It's raining like a pisser," he laughed, "but you can actually see some sunshine out at sea. That a good sign?"

I smiled. Since Barry had learned yesterday that he was actually going to be making a passage in an ocean-going sailboat, he had become insatiably curious about all aspects of nautical life. I had tried to give him an overview on the weather problems we'd been having, but he wanted a more detailed explanation. This tentative discussion had inevitably expanded to the point where I found myself in the middle of an hour-long lecture on basic meteorology. Now I realized that I wasn't going to escape with some noncommital comment about the current weather.

Rising, I pulled on my jacket. "Let me just go have a peek at what the sky and the barometer are doing," I said. "You finish my chess game with Doug."

Barry nodded earnestly. He seemed pleased to have been given this assignment.

I snapped up the front of my jacket and went out to the café steps to wait out the current downpour under the stone portico of the old Venetian warehouse. Barry was right about the clear sky out to sea.

Northwest of the green shoulder of the nearby cape, blue afternoon sky was ripping long rents in the heavy overcast. Here in the closed harbor, the wind still swirled, but the violence of the rain was visibly decreasing. Soon the downpour was a drizzle, then a fine mist. Now the sun actually touched the stone walls of the old Turkish fortifications above the harbor.

Leaving the shelter of the portico, I strolled along the dock to clear my head after the brandy and the smoky heat of the café. It was pleasant to be alone after the rough passage from Malta. Tomorrow, there'd be four of us aboard *Matata* and the quarters would be even tighter. Now I had the chance to get some exercise and to simply enjoy being in Greece again.

With the end of the rain, the harbor front seemed to come back to life. A long blue caique crossed the boat basin and moored alongside, several boat lengths up from us. As if mustered by an unseen drill sergeant, men left the nearby cafés and ouzo bars and ambled over to the fishing boat to examine their catch. Many of the men on the pier seemed to be fishermen themselves, and others looked like stevedores or the drivers of the big Mercedes and Daimler trucks that were lined up in a tight pack, their muddy tarpaulins almost touching, at the far end of the pier. They were waiting for a ferryboat that had been delayed by the storm.

As I watched the watchers, they assembled in a loose formation at the edge of the quay and stared down at the men in the caique. Several of the men on the quay twirled strings of amber worry beads, others feigned disinterest by slowly loading cigarette holders and lighting the cigarettes for each other with elaborate butane lighters. There was, I knew, an archaic Mediterranean ritual being enacted before me. If the crews of the trucks could effectively employ their urban wiles, they might be able to buy a kilo or two of fresh *barbounia* at a bargain price from the local bumpkins. Once they had the fish, the drivers could easily prevail on the café owners to fry the fish and chop up some cucumber and tomatoes for *salata horiatiki*.

But the fishermen certainly understood the exact nature of the charade being enacted above them. For their part, the fishermen showed absolutely no awareness that these burly long-distance truckers were even watching. The caique's skipper, an old man in a patched olive-drab deck coat—probably liberated from the German Navy, thirty-five years earlier—stopped to hoist a long open fish crate onto the edge of the pier. The crate was filled with cracked ice and long rows of fresh, pink *barbounia*, the small red mullet of the Aegean that the Greeks prize above all other fish.

"Dimitri," the old man bellowed, his voice echoing off the warehouse arches, "Dimitri, *ella 'tho me ton karotzaki sou.*"

He was calling a man named Dimitri to bring his three-wheeled delivery scooter.

This was an excellent ploy that momentarily thwarted the assembled truckers. If the skipper had acknowledged their presence, they might have been able to wait for him to make the first direct overtures about the availability and price of the fish. Now he had called their bluff. If they didn't act, he actually would send this whole crate of *barbounia* up the hill to the tavernas in the upper town.

The putt-putt stammer of a Zündapp three-wheeler grew louder as the rickety scooter lurched toward us through the puddles. With practiced skill, the skipper turned his back on the truckers and bent to tinker with his rusty engine controls inside the caique's weather-ravaged doghouse.

Before the Zündapp arrived at the side of the quay, one of the drivers, a handsome fellow who affected an Austrian loden coat over the shoulders of his mechanic's coveralls, broke th tension by directly addressing the skipper. Now the bargaining was officially begun. In a moment the preliminary exchange between the tall driver and the skipper had evolved into a boisterous, animated, and seemingly hostile group debate that occupied all the men on the pier and the three fishermen in the boat. Hands were thrust forward, palms up, wrists parallel, mute emphasis to indicate the opponents were talking unmitigated nonsense. Fingers were wagged. Feet stamped. One driver turned abruptly to stride away, then turned back, both hands waving.

The fishermen were shouting a slurred Kritiaki that I found almost incomprehensible. For their part, the truckers had reverted to the stylized guttural slang of the Piraeus waterfront *manges*. One of the few phrases I could consistently distinguish was, "*Okhi, malaka!*" 'No, you masturbator!"

Any tourist unfamiliar with Greece, I knew, would view this scene as an ugly confrontation among potentially violent workingmen on an isolated dock. But, of course, violence and anger were utterly absent from the exchange. This was pleasure, what Nikos Kazantzakis, the famous Cretan novelist, once called the "free honey" of a spirited public argument.

As I ambled off down the quay toward town, the counterfeit outrage and vituperation rose and fell behind me. More than the tarry retsina we'd drunk for lunch, more than the mousaka of last night's dinner, this mock *fassaria* between the fishermen and the big-city truckers brought home to me the splendid truth that we were actually back in Greece. We had managed to sail our small boat from another isolated dock—Danny Dimeglio's Boatyard in Brooklyn, where, for good reason, arguments were taken much more seriously—to this medieval stone pier where men could strut and display their *philotimou* with such charming, predictable grandiosity.

I was whistling now as I strode along, the harsh, touching theme music from *Zorba the Greek*.

FROM HANIA TO SITIA at the eastern end of Crete is only 125 miles, but it was the wettest, most uncomfortable passage I have ever experienced. Poor Barry downed the Dramamine I handed out all around but was unable to rise from his bunk. His robust young body was laid low, although he attempted to eat the concoction of crackers and bouillon I prepared for him. After the first swallow, he literally turned green and groaned in his misery. "I can't *believe* anyone would do this for fun!"

I hung by one hand from the grab rail, balancing a mug of soup in the churning cabin. If I didn't get topside soon myself, I too would be turning green. I checked the canvas leeboard that prevented Barry from being thrown out of his bunk, assured him it would get better, then struggled back into my oilskins.

Before leaving Hania we had obtained a fair-weather forecast from the U.S. Navy and NATO base at Soudha Bay. The sky *did* look like it was going to clear, but that had been several hours earlier. When we'd rounded the cape after leaving Hania, we'd been hit by a strong force five out of the east. And there was a swell running down on us from the northeast, pushing us toward that rocky coast of Crete. Now it was raining. No question about it, we had a proper sirocco blowing and we were trying to sail right into the teeth of it. Even with the engine on at high revs, we were making little headway. But we *were* continuing east slowly, and Mal and I decided to tough it out. For now, we had the tall, mountainous island of Crete to the south of us, shielding us from the worst of the squalls. Unless conditions improved, however, we would have to stop again, at Sitia, rather than attempt the Kassos-Crete channel open to the full power of the sirocco.

Our taste of Greece at Hania had made Malcolm and me anxious to get home, back to Lindos, where we had lived for several years, to the many friends we had there, both Greek and *xenie*, foreigners like ourselves who made their home in this pretty, quiet village for part of each year.

"You know," I said to Malcolm when I finally negotiated the leaping maneuver that took me from the dry companionway, over the storm boards, into the very wet cockpit, "even the weather is Greek—boisterous and threatening."

"But great sailing, right?" Malcolm was grinning at me under the snugged-down yellow hood of his oilskin. I hadn't seen him so happy in more than a month . . . not since—I tried to remember—since we had arrived in the Azores! *So what*, I knew he meant, *so what if it's cold and wet and the boat thinks its a roller coaster, we're back in Greece; we're almost home.*

But enough is enough. We holed up in Sitia the next afternoon.

It is amazing how quickly a person suffering from seasickness can recover as soon as he steps on firm, unmoving land. Barry was a dramatic example of this recuperative power. Within an hour of our arrival in Sitia, he had arranged a table for us at a local taverna for the evening; he wanted to celebrate his first sailing voyage. I noticed, however, that he wasn't anxious to come back on board for a rest before dinner.

That night, a Saturday, the small taverna was packed with a wedding party as well as the few foreigners washed up at this isolated port in Crete. Barry, naturally, invited a couple of young Cretan men to join us for a glass of ouzo at our table. Soon two were giving an exhibition of the *syrtaki*, jumping and spinning in the air in unison as their compatriot thumped his bouzouki. But, as much as we enjoyed the evening ashore, Mal and I decided we'd better go back to the boat early. It was raining much harder suddenly, and even inside the restaurant you could tell from the rattle of the windowpanes that the wind was increasing.

The sirocco blew for two days, two more days of delay on our passage to Lindos. But with *Matata* snug in this well-protected harbor, and good friends to help while away the time, we made the best of it and settled down to seriously enjoy our return to Greece.

CHAPTER ELEVEN

NOVEMBER 1, MORNING
LINDOS, RHODES

When Carol called me, I was wedged head first in the starboard quarterberth, trying to steal an hour's sleep after the long, pounding night. I knew from the tone of her voice that we had a problem. Scuttling backward like a lobster in my carapace of salty oilskins and safety harness, I extracted myself from the berth and threw back the companionway hatch.

It was a dull, cloudy morning with a good 35 knots blowing from the northwest. The boat was heeled sharply as we beat north under reefed main and storm jib. Carol was at the tiller, straining against the weight of the weather helm. Doug crouched on the lowside, getting some shelter from the cold spray, and poor Barry was sprawled like a wounded soldier in the monsoon rain, his awkward rubber poncho flailing about his face. We only had three sets of oilskins aboard, and none of them would fit Barry. A quick look around told me he'd been seasick again.

I pushed past him as gently as I could, and he groaned something unintelligible. Using the swaying end of the boom as a brace, I dragged myself upright to look around. Ahead of us the dark hump of Cape Prasonisi, the southern extremity of Rhodes, stood gray-green under the sullen overcast. I'd been asleep for longer than I thought. We were only 5 or 6 miles from the bottom of the island, only 25 from Lindos.

In my thick fatigue, I gazed stupidly at the green curve of land, unable to fully grasp that what I was seeing represented the end of a voyage almost one-third of the way around the planet.

"Jesus," I finally muttered, "the cape . . . that's Rhodes . . . "

Carol cut short my dreamy rambling. "Malcolm, look under the jib." Her voice was clear and low, as it always was when there was danger. "There's a freighter out there on a collision course."

Instantly my clotted lethargy burned away in a hot rush of alarm. I shouldered Doug back on the bench so that I could lean over the starboard rail and peer ahead. As the boat smacked down into each angular swell, I got a fractured view of the ship bearing down on us, about 20 degrees off the starboard bow. It was a fast, modern general-cargo freighter with curved superstructure well aft and some red containers stacked on the main deck. It looked about a mile away, and closing at 20 knots.

"Get ready to tack," I said, thrusting past the wet tangle of Barry's poncho to take the tiller.

"Wait a second," Carol said. Her tone was strained now with fear and frustration. "I tacked ten minutes ago, but this goddamn current just knocked us back. We'll have to start the engine."

"Okay," I muttered, trying to sound calm. "Doug, you go down and prime it, then hit the circuit breaker. Barry, you'll have to make some room for us here when we tack."

Barry mumbled again and drew in his sprawling limbs.

I slipped around Carol on the highside cockpit coaming and took the wet teak weight of the tiller. We were in the Karpathos Strait, the channel separating Rhodes from its southern neighbor. Greek fishermen called this channel the Devil's Strait because of the wild currents and the dangerous, hollow sea that built up in a northwest blow like this.

Carol eased herself down next to Barry and got the sheet coils squared away to tack. I heard the engine rumble into life under my feet and eased the throttle back to fast idle. We'd been having trouble with the waterpump in the past two days of powering, and it wouldn't be a good idea to use the engine in this current until I was sure we had cooling water out the exhaust. After about thirty seconds, I strained and twisted backward as well as I could, still keeping one hand on the tiller, to check for a spout of cooling water at the exhaust port beneath me.

There was gray smoke, a few wisps of steam, but sure as hell, no pulsing spurts of water. *Shit,* I thought, *why now?*

"*Malcolm,*" Carol said in her overly calm emergency-nobody-panic voice. "The ship. He's . . . "

Her words were lost in the multiple blast of the freighter's horn, a shocking domination of sound that made my flesh crawl.

Fighting the edges of panic, I reached down and jammed the engine gear lever full forward and followed it with the throttle full open. If we burnt out a valve by overheating, I knew, it was better than getting rammed by that freighter. "We're not going to tack," I yelled to Carol. But the freighter's horn blasted again. I wanted to tell her that tacking over to power up against the current was a bad maneuver, with the engine not one hundred percent reliable. My intention was to bear off downwind on sail and engine.

She sprang to the sheet winch and let the coil fly. What she had heard in my words was, "We're *going* to tack." The jib flogged noisily. Carol spun to face me, her eyes shocked and angry when I did not head up.

"We're *not* tacking," I yelled. "No . . . negative. We're falling off." Gesturing wildly at the traveler, I shouted, "Ease the main sheet . . . *fast.*"

She recovered her wits at once. The main billowed out onto a beam reach and she pounced on the snapping jib sheet that was only held from runaway by a loose figure-eight knot in the track block. The bow plowed around through the white crests until we had the cold northwest wind dead on the port beam. At this point of sailing, the freighter was clearly visible, a tall rusty wall of white metal that cut a ragged bow wave through the swells. I couldn't be sure of the distance, with my heart thudding in my chest and my breath coming in hot gasps. But I knew he wasn't more than two hundred yards away.

Barry groaned once more, this time a sorrowful moan well mixed with fear. I was close to joining him. Ten seconds later, I could see the freighter's bow bear off, 5 degrees, now 15, then 20. He was going to miss us by fifty yards.

As the ship passed, Doug emerged from the companionway, Barry vomited, and Carol said something about the engine racing. Poor Barry's poncho once more had snagged on the engine controls, dragging the gear lever into neutral with the throttle wide open. In the thirty seconds of shouting confusion that ensued, the ship trundled by and was gone, leaving behind a sooty stench of stack gas and a pressure wave that almost pooped us.

Once we got the crowded cockpit squared away and I was able to verify that we were now, indeed, getting adequate cooling water through the engine, the ship was practically a mile away.

"Anybody see a name or a flag on that guy?" I asked. "I'd like to write the skipper an apology letter."

Doug shook his head. Barry only groaned, and spit up some beige foam. "It happened too fast," Carol added.

"It sure did," I said. "He was going about 30 knots."

"Doesn't he realize that there's an energy crisis?" Doug said in his best outraged citizen voice. "I've half a mind to report him to Jimmy Carter."

Carol and I laughed weakly. Barry slumped in his place and grunted.

I could feel the usual spongy tingling in my limbs from another dangerous encounter. "What time is it?" My voice was flat, sleepy again.

"About ten to nine," Doug said.

"Once we go on the other tack," I said, "I will hereby declare the sun over this bucket's yardarm. . . . Is there any brandy left, or did you lushes finish it off last night when you were supposed to be keeping watch?"

Carol stopped coiling down the jib sheet, stood shakily to look around the somber, crashing seascape, and pulled herself toward the hatch. "I know where the bottle is," she said.

By 1030, we'd killed the brandy and had started on a bottle of Marko retsina. We were in flat water now, about six miles south of Pefkos Point and only three off the gravel beaches at Gennadion. Inland, there were thick rolls of gray rain cloud hiding the four-thousand-foot ridgeline of Prophet Elias. Ahead, the Lindos Acropolis stood out delicately against the thunderheads further up the island. The wind had backed almost due west and steadied at 25 knots. Between the last brandy and the first of the retsina, Doug and I had gone up to the foredeck and hoisted the working jib. Now the boat hissed along at a smooth 7 knots.

Half an hour later, Carol passed up some cheese and a tin of French paté that she'd been hoarding for our arrival. Before I ate, however, I carefully cleaned the lenses of the binoculars with fresh water and soft tissue paper. I felt swelling within me a definite sense of unreality, an inability to believe that those rainy green mountains, that unmistakable headland was actually Rhodes, our immutable goal for all these months on the sea. Once I cleaned the binoculars, I wedged in close to the main traveler and steadied my elbow on the coachroof to provide a solid support for the glasses.

Lindos hung clear and white, the houses bright cubes filling the saddle between the island's eastern slope and the brown, stony rectangle of the Acropolis. This was no postcard, no half-remembered dream image. We were five miles from the village and closing fast. I handed Doug the glasses, and he and Barry indulged themselves in the usual superlatives about the beauty of the setting, the drama of the terraced white village, and the overhanging colonnade of ruins above on the Acropolis.

Carol was still, silent at the helm, watching the village draw closer. I couldn't judge her emotions, as I usually could. I wondered if she was in as much of a muddle as me.

Suddenly I found myself busy with small boat-keeping details. I was up on the foredeck, lashing down perfectly secure bits of tackle, then striding aft with the salty bundle of the bagged storm jib. Before taking the sailbag below, I untied the bucket lanyard and took the plastic pail with me. Stopping, I realized what I was doing. Aside from externalizing the almost unbearable joy, the hot flood of pride that welled within me, I saw that I was also preparing the boat, *Matata,* for its mooring, just as I had done so many times before outside Lindos Bay with *Piraya* or *Kormoran.* But this was another boat, this was our own small ocean cruiser, our passage maker that had carried us almost seven thousand miles in five months, across the gray void of the North Atlantic, through the Strait to Gib, on to the Balearics, to Carlo Forte, to Marsala, where we waited out the storm lashed to the trawlers, to the fantasy dawn landfall at Malta, to the misty cape of Crete . . . all that endless, headwind-tormented slog, all the doubts and confusing night approaches, all that weather. It seemed clearly impossible that the task was now ended, that the passage was over, the journey complete.

I dropped through the hatch and stowed the sail and bucket in the forepeak. Then I went to work folding and stowing the damp clothes we'd strewn around the cabin in the past day and night. Next, I rolled the sleeping bags tight and jammed them into their tote bags for the first time in five months. Working slowly, absolutely absorbed with the task, I squared away below decks. Our boat was now ready to receive all our Lindos friends . . . Peter, Uli and Heinz, Klaus and Erika, John O'Kane and his artist mother, Doris. We were almost *home,* and our small ship was ready.

"Malcolm," Carol called; now her voice was languid, almost hesitant. "There's something you really ought to see up here."

I realized from her tone that the "something" was Lindos. But I was not in the least prepared for what I saw when I climbed to the cockpit. I blinked painfully in the hot wash of sunlight. While I'd been below decks, the wind had backed southwest, and the dour weight of overcast had been shredded. Now the sky was a booming cobalt, a *Vora* sky that often came after a cold northerly. The rain had washed the atmosphere. We could see clearly north, six capes up toward Rhodes City. Inland, the green parallel ridges rose from the coast, all the way to the cedar forests of Prophet Elias.

Lindos was balanced there between the green hills and the glaring rock of the Acropolis, white, clean, silent.

The sun beat like a trumpet on my strangely wet cheeks.

Washington, 1984

APPENDIX

1. MEDITERRANEAN WEATHER PATTERNS

When Carol and I came to live in Greece in the late 1960s, we were already familiar with the climate of Morocco, at the opposite end of the Mediterranean. We had only sailed there as neophyte crew on other people's boats, however, and never ventured further than a few miles from Tangier. Naturally, we understood that the local winter levanters could be dangerous for small boats when we read the lurid accounts in the French-language press of fishing trawlers sinking, but we had an image of the Aegean as a gentle, sun-washed lake from our previous visits there.

Our first year in Lindos, we were more involved with writing books than with sailing, so our interest in the local weather patterns retained a typical landsman's orientation. We were not yet sailors and hadn't learned to search the sea and sky for important clues to the impending weather. That next spring we began to crew on the large charter yawl *Kormoran* and quickly came to realize that Mediterranean weather was often violent and unpredictable.

As discussed in chapter 5, the intensity of winds in the Mediterranean is a function of the sea's location between two climatically different land masses and of the unique topography of the littoral regions. Further, the weather patterns in the Western and Eastern Basins also differ due to size and shape of these basins and the land forms of their coasts.

The Western Basin is considerably smaller than the Eastern, and the western "half" is almost completely surrounded by mountains. On the southern coast, the Atlas Range stretches from the Rif of Morocco all the way to Tunisia's Djebel Nementcha, where the blood-soaked Kasserine Pass of World War II infamy offers one of the few direct connections from the Sahara to the sea. Spain's coastal *sierras* form an unbroken wall from Gibraltar through Andalucia and Valencia to Catalonia, where the Pyrenees seal off the Spanish coast from French Languedoc and the Rhone delta. After the "slot" of the Rhône valley, the Maritime Alps meld with the Apennines, which then march the length of the Italian peninsula, jump the Straits of Messina, and join the volcanic highlands of Sicily. Corsica and Sardinia, as well as the Balearic Islands, are also mountain barriers around or over which the surface winds and air masses must channel themselves as they obey the imperatives of thermodynamics and the Coriolis Effect.

When one considers the mountain-locked nature of the western Med, it is not surprising that that region's two best-known wind systems—the mistral of the Rhône Valley and the levanter that dominates the Strait of Gibraltar—blow with such intensity. I once asked an experienced British yacht captain, Paul Adamthwaite, who had sailed on all the oceans of the world, where he had experienced the worst storm of his thirty-year career.

"The Med," he'd answered without hesitation, "a mistral in September, south of Marseilles. Had a Brooks and Gatehouse anenometer pegged at sixty knots for thirty hours. Clear sky, absolute bugger of a sea, and that frigid bloody *wall* of a wind."

"What did you do?" I asked, knowing he must have employed some effective tactic or otherwise wouldn't have been sitting next to me at the bar in St. Barts, drinking a bottle of Heineken.

"Lay ahull and drifted south, helm lashed down hard. Drifted for thirty-some hours at about five knots. Mind you, not a thread of canvas on her, and we were driven to leeward at an average speed of *five* knots. That's what the mistral will do to you if it decides to have a bit of fun."

Given the Venturi Effect on compressable fluids, such as our planet's atmosphere, I now understand why the mistral can be so savage. If the area through which a given volume of wind must pass is constricted, as in the Rhône Valley, the velocity of that wind will increase. This principle works equally in the region of Gibraltar; only sixty miles separate the eight-thousand-foot ridge of the Moroccan Rif from the eleven-thousand-foot summits of Spain's Sierra Nevada. When there is a deep depression offshore in the Atlantic, all the easterly flow of wind must compress itself through the narrow Venturi tube of the strait.

The dominant weather of the western Med, aside from the mistral and levanter, is the so-called Genoa Low or lee cyclone. On meteorological maps, a secondary, or "Mediterranean," depression will often develop in the Gulf of Genoa when the cold front of a continental low to the north swings southeast across the Tyrrhenian Sea, over the Malta Channel and into the open water of the Eastern Basin.

When this occurs—usually during the five months of the eastern zone's rainy season from November through April—conditions are right for the sudden, violent sirocco gales that sometimes reach the scale of mini-hurricanes as they churn eastward across the Ionian, Libyan, and Aegean seas. Depending on the latitude of the maritime depression's center, the storm will unleash most of its violent energy on either the Adriatic/Ionian area or the southern Aegean and Sea of Crete.

Often in the autumn or spring, the thermal gradient between East Europe and the North African coast is most severe. This radical difference in temperatures sometimes leads to an extremely steep barometric pressure gradient surrounding a Mediterranean depression. On one recent April weather chart there was a low in the Ionian Sea with a 1,002-millibar center and a 1,036-millibar high in the Danube Valley, only four hundred miles to the northwest. The low was driven east into the Aegean, bringing with it force nine northeast gales above the Cyclades and a force eight southeast sirocco that battered the Dodecanese. This sudden gale drove ashore a large American charter ketch, whose skipper had unwisely sought refuge in Lindos harbor, an anchorage that is wide open to the smashing southeast swell.

Again, the Venturi Effect of the mountain barrier that blocks the northern shore of the entire Mediterranean intensified the wind force. And the six-hundred-mile fetch of the open sea from Rhodes to the Levant also increased the size and power of the swells that ripped the American yacht off its mooring and smashed it on the Lindos beach.

The New Testament and the legends of the Greek Orthodox Church are replete with stories of Saint Paul and other Apostles preaching the gospel being driven ashore by savage winter storms all over Asia minor, the Greek islands, and southern Italy. Usually, legend has it that the Lord intervened at the last possible moment and cleaved asunder the rocks protecting a harbor—just enough to allow safe entrance to the Roman grain ship on which the apostle was a passenger—but not enough to admit the destructive power of the southern swell. In fact, Saint Paul's Bay on the southeast corner of the Lindos acropolis promontory is one of these sites of miraculous salvation from imminent foundering on a rock-bound lee shore. The bay has two narrow entrances, one possibly large enough for a hundred-ton Roman grain vessel to pass through. Once inside, however, the ship wouldn't have lasted long. Saint Paul's bay is like a high-speed washing machine when the sirocco swell surges through and the successive waves work on each other. The anchorage is shallow, and the rocky bottom offers poor holding. If Saint Paul did make it through the narrow pass, he probably got his feet wet before the day was over.

The etesian or summer winds of the Eastern Basin are dominated by the Aegean meltemi. As noted in chapter 5, this is a strong "slot" wind system analogous to the mistral. What makes the meltemi more of a problem for the yacht sailor than its western analogue, however, is the topography of the Aegean archipelago. On the French Riviera, you might be driven offshore by a sudden *coup de mistral* and end up spending the whole afternoon on a chill beat to windward, back to your anchorage at Toulon or Hyeres. But in the Aegean, yachts driven before a slashing force eight meltemi will find hundreds of very solid islands, islets, and unlighted rocks blocking their escape to leeward.

Strategy therefore becomes of great importance for yacht sailors cruising the Aegean. Sailing in Greece is a little like balloon flying; a balloonist is always jealous of giving up altitude that he's *paid* for with either propane fuel or ballast. The sailor making his way across the summer Aegean should always be jealous of relinquishing his northerly position, because usually he's had to *buy* that position with hard slogs into the chill, salty teeth of the meltemi. As I outlined in chapter 5, wise charter skippers have evolved tactics that include pre-dawn departures and motor-sailing up the narrow channels separating the Dodecanese Islands and Turkey or the scattered islands of the Cyclades. The meltemi, being dependent on thermal-barometric gradients between East Europe and the Levant, rarely blows hard for the two or three hours before and after sunrise. That's the time to make good the northern leg of your day's passage. Then, when the meltemi starts to puff, you can reach across it east or west and, in the process, experience some of the best sailing in the world.

The yacht sailor cruising the Mediterranean for the first time should definitely bear in mind the nature of the region's weather patterns, then make certain prudent additions to his cruise plan.

First, those sailing the summer Aegean should consider the meltemi. It is unrealistic to plan on long northerly or northwesterly passages during the full meltemi season—from mid-June to mid-September. This is especially true for bareboat charters who begin in Piraeus, sail southeast into the Cyclades, then are faced with the long beat back against the meltemi. It's even worse for those who ride the wind all the way down to Crete or Rhodes and have only two or three days left of their charter to recoup the 180 miles back to the mainland. In Greece, in the summer, it's well to remember that you can average twice as far downwind during your cruise than you can beating into the short, pounding meltemi sea.

Secondly, anyone sailing the Med should remember that the equinox periods are often some of the stormiest times of the year. If you're going to take advantage of cheap off-season bareboat rates, especially in Greece and Italy, be prepared to spend part of your cruise stormbound in harbor.

Which leads to the third principle: locate adequate storm shelter harbors along your intended routes—safe, all-weather safe havens, not simply anchorages that offer protection from one direction. When a Mediterranean depression churns across the Ionian or the Aegean, the gale force wind will often veer around from northeast to southeast in a matter of hours. Keep in mind the unfortunate captain of the USS *Bache*, whose destroyer was pounded to pieces on the Rhodes breakwater, or the imprudent American yacht skipper who left his ketch in Lindos harbor while he took his crew to dinner up in the village. When they rolled down the hill at midnight, their boat was being battered in the surf.

These days, however, the advent of accurate weather forecasts based on meteorological satellite coverage has been a boon to the Mediterranean sailor. Local maritime forecasts have also improved considerably in the past five years. Whenever I sail in the Med, I follow a strict weather-forecast discipline, even if it means interrupting a dinner party. I always try to watch the local evening television news weather forecast to catch the latest satellite picture of the region. This way, I can track the progress and intensity of approaching depressions or highs. I also take careful notes when I listen to the local maritime forecasts, which are usually broadcast in English early each morning in France, Italy, and Greece. Any sailor coming to cruise the Med should obtain an up-to-date schedule of maritime weather forecasts for the area he intends to sail, and also plan to watch the local television news each night in waterfront cafés.

Naturally, I also keep a close eye on the sky signs and the barometer. In this manner, I've come to better understand the annual patterns that dominate the region's climate. These rhythms, I now realize, are old and predictable. They've been controlling the lives of Mediterranean seafarers for centuries.

I'll never forget the stories old Georgas the fisherman told me that first year we lived in Lindos. Georgas was already in his late seventies when we met him. As a boy, he had gone to sea on the large cargo caiques that then carried much of the freight across the Eastern Mediterranean. These were beamy, shallow-draft gaff-riggers. The larger craft were schooner rigged, some with up to three masts, the mizzen usually carrying a smaller triangular lateen sail. As Georgas explained, the crew of any given caique worked as a cooperative company, each man buying in his share of the cargo—or, more likely, borrowing from a money lender to purchase a mortgaged share of eventual profits. The captain was the chief stockholder and, of course, absolute monarch aboard.

Each season, the captain tried to start as far north as was practical. In the case of Georgas's vessel, they usually began the year in Smyrna, the present-day Izmir, which was the center of the large Greek coastal enclave in Ottoman Turkey. Their usual cargo was timber for the Greek mainland, and they would complete as many trips as they could in the spring and early summer, until the meltemi drove them south. Then, perhaps with a cargo of wool or dried fruit, they would ride the prevailing northerlies down the Anatolian coast to Cyprus and on to Palestine. By autumn, they were often in Alexandria, ready to carry baled Egyptian cotton north on the sirocco, all the way back to Smyrna. When becalmed, he said, they towed the caique with a long boat, rowing six-hour shifts.

Georgas in his seventies was stooped and wrinkled. But he was still strong in bone and muscle. His face was tanned and wind-battered to the texture of harness leather. His fingers were deeply scarred by fifty years of rough hempline. He retired from the sea in the 1950s and took up the less challenging work of fishing the local waters to supply the tables of his grown children and typically large extended family. He never forgot the years he had spent aboard those ponderous but graceful sailing craft, riding the planet's annual rhythms of meltemi and sirocco across the ancient face of the Middle Sea.

When we reached Lindos aboard *Matata* in November 1979, one of the first people we met on the old stone jetty was Georgas. He had tears on his face as he embraced us. We were, he proclaimed *"megali capitanos,"* great captains, to have sailed our own boat all the way from America to Lindos. No one else in the village would understand, he added gravely; they were not sailors. But he, Georgas, who had been at sea all those long decades, he understood what we had seen and felt and lived on the days and nights at sea.

Georgas died quietly in his sleep three years later. That last summer, he was too short of breath to make the walk down the long track from the village to the boat landing beneath the limestone bluff of the acropolis. But he would often sit in the shade of the plane tree in the *platea*, smiling out at the meltemi's white scroll on the blue face of the Aegean.

2. MEDITERRANEAN MOORING AND ISLAND ANCHORAGES

O ne of the most vexing problems facing the yacht sailor on his first Mediterranean cruise is the widespread practice of stern-to mooring in crowded yacht basins. This problem is especially severe in Greece, where marina development has been slow, but the south of France is also a challenge. Most Americans and British sailors are used to either tying up in slips or anchoring in a bay and taking a dinghy ashore. This is not possible in traditional Mediterranean ports. The yacht basins are often narrow pens between quays of low cement block or old dressed stone construction. And there are so many yachts vying for space along the quayside that everyone must stern-to with warps ashore and a bow anchor out.

Therein lies the problem. Sailboats are not designed to travel well astern, especially when there's a strong meltemi or mistral puffing down the bluff above the harbor and the opening into which the boat

205

is being maneuvered is only slightly wider than her beam. I've seen some memorable scenes of frustration and bitter acrimony—often between husbands and wives—when a newcomer to the Med tries to moor in a crowded harbor.

Over the years, the early ones of which were equally trying for me and Carol, we have slowly learned how to stern-to to a crowded quay. Once understood, the techniques are not difficult to practice.

First, you have to remember that sailboats do not *easily* steer when going astern. This problem is exacerbated when the anchor is down and the chain running out creates a drag at the bow. And, of course, there's a damn *gale* blowing off the quay to push your exposed stern downwind from your intended track. To overcome these problems, it's best to employ either of the following tactics:

First, you must get the boat moving reasonably fast astern so that you can actually *steer* it with reverse movements of the tiller or wheel. This may mean that you'll have to promenade backward about the harbor for a few minutes as the boat drives itself in a cockeyed circle until there is finally enough water-flow across the rudder to allow steady steering. A mistake a lot of novices make is to simply throw the gear lever astern a short distance out from the quay and *hope* that the boat will steer well astern. This rarely happens. Once the boat *is* steering well, I slow down to a speed that permits minimum way against the wind, line up the transom with the intended spot on the quay, and ask Carol to drop the anchor while still far enough upwind to prevent drifting down on the boat moored to leeward.

Naturally, we have a pair of stern warps already cleated on and coiled for throwing, and as many fenders down on each side as we feel are needed. As I steer the boat backward, Carol pays out the anchor line until I'm within heaving distance with a stern warp. After I have a line fixed ashore, she digs the anchor in, and I take up the tension with the windward stern warp. After that, it's a simple matter of winching ourselves up to the quay on our warps, tightening the anchor line—or slacking it—as required, and breaking out the ouzo for a sundowner in the cockpit.

The alternate technique is just a variation of the one above. Instead of dropping the anchor while going astern, line the *bow* up with the desired spot on the pier, drop the hook, then power around it, digging in the anchor in the process. Start to go astern when the boat swings around over its own anchor chain. At this point, with the person at the anchor giving plenty of slack, use adequate throttle to get water flowing across the rudder blade and gain steering control astern. After that, follow the same system as outlined above.

Now I must mention the problems of anchor fouling in crowded Mediterranean harbors. This is a perennial headache, especially as large power boats often drop two anchors and drag them badly around the bottom as they maneuver astern. Even if you've been careful about not crossing anybody's chain when you dropped, you might end up with a couple 100-pound CQRs across yours when you leave in the morning. As anyone who's been unlucky enough to suffer this can attest, dragging up a big chain and anchor is no fun and can be downright dangerous to backs, toes, and fingers unless the maneuver is done correctly.

Often the weight of the fouled chain is too much for a small electric anchor winch. I've learned to reinforce the anchor winch with a headsail halyard winch mounted on the mast. What I do is simply snap the clip of my wire jib halyard as far down my own chain as I can reach by leaning under the bow pulpit, and use the two winches together to drag up the offending chain. Then I double-off a thick line to hold the chain to our bow, slack our own anchor and stow it, slack the halyard, then slip the end of the doubled-off line and sail away. Until I learned this trick, I suffered a lot of strained backs and bent boat hooks, wrestling with rusty chains.

Naturally, you won't anchor each night in a port when you cruise the Mediterranean. Much of your time will be spent in bays. Unfortunately, some of the more popular bays are so deep and steep-bottomed that you won't be able to swing freely on an anchor but must ride on a bow anchor with stern warps ashore. As with Med mooring, there are techniques to make this an easy maneuver.

I usually drop a short, temporary anchor—often only a ten-pound grapple—then take the dinghy ashore with a long stern warp, which I double-off through a short loop of "sacrificial" line that I've tied around a suitable rock or tree. That way, the loop gets the chafe, not my good line, and, if necessary, I can simply slip one end of the double warp and sail free—without the hassle of having to go ashore again to free my stern. Once the stern warp is tied, I use the dinghy to drop a longer, permanent anchor. This way I can place it well upwind, vis-à-vis my position relative to the shore.

As many of the Greek and Turkish bays mentioned in the popular cruising guides are ancient harbors, there is usually one part of the anchorage that offers the best protection from the prevailing winds and swell. As often as not, the local fishermen know these spots. You can see their colorful boats clustered with anchors and shore moorings in a part of the harbor that initially might not seem convenient to you. Chances are, however, that centuries of experience with the prevailing weather have taught the local people where they can most safely anchor. In a strange bay, I will always follow the local fishermen's lead, if I have a choice.

If there are no such obvious clues, I try to imagine a worst-case scenario, especially in the changeable weather of the spring or autumn. There is rarely a television set available in a secluded bay to bring me a satellite picture of the impending weather, so I always try to seek shelter from a potential wind shift or unexpected swell. This habit comes from several seasons skippering a charterboat in the Aegean. When you have paying guests on board, you hate to ruin their sleep with the hassle and commotion of shifting anchor in the middle of the night; equally, you become more safety-conscious when you are carrying passengers.

To avoid overcrowded summer anchorages, I learned years ago to tuck into the smallest possible creeks and crannies, again employing a long double stern warp ashore and a deep, heavy anchor placed from the dinghy. During the so-called settled weather of the Mediterranean summer, a system of sea and land breezes usually prevails between bouts of the dominant etesian wind, be it the mistral, the meltemi, or the bora of the Adriatic. When these stronger winds do not blow for several days—usually due to a stagnant high in the region—sea and land "breezes" can develop into quite respectable winds, certainly strong enough to kick up an uncomfortable chop in an exposed anchorage or lead to puffy afternoon downdrafts off cliffs when the land effect takes over. When anchoring in a bay or narrow creek, I always weigh the possibility of sea and land breezes against the prevailing wind system before setting my mooring. Such advance planning might seem like annoying work for sailors used to the marinas of Long Island Sound or the snug anchorages of the Solent. But Carol and I don't mind the extra effort. We have spent some of the most pleasurable moments of our life afloat, tucked into narrow mini-fjords on the Turquoise Coast of Anatolia. The surrounding ridges are dense with olive trees and maritime pines, the head of the inlet often a clean white beach, only fifty feet long. Sometimes there's a granite sarcophagus or Hellenistic tomb perched on the shoulder of the nearby headland. The air is clean and spicy with pine, and the deep water beneath the keel is that rich, luminous blue that one can never capture in words, or even on film. In the evening the squat owls of Athena drift down to hunt among the trees, their calls a mournful, evocative chime. At times like this, which we've enjoyed every summer since sailing our boat to Greece, we do not miss the bustle and efficiency of a modern marina.

3. SEAMANSHIP IN MEDITERRANEAN CONDITIONS

My personal weather log for the past eleven years indicates that the waters of the eastern Aegean have been calm with light breezes on the average of 42 percent of the days during the May through October sailing season. From June 15 to September 15 during this same period, however, northwest winds of force five and above have prevailed 60 percent of the time. As most foreign sailors cruise Greece in midsummer, either aboard their own yachts or on bareboat charters, they can therefore probably expect to contend with the meltemi about six days out of ten.

The mistral in southern France is less regular but tends to blow harder when it does rise, and the bora of the Adriatic is a regular feature of the spring and autumn sailing seasons. As mentioned earlier, "Mediterranean front" depressions can be expected about once a week during the five-month winter rainy season. What all these wind systems have in common is their dramatic effect on local sea conditions.

I've met a number of American and British yacht sailors who have been shocked by the difficulty they've had facing the short, steep "pyramid" sea of the Mediterranean in a bad mistral, meltemi or sirocco. Sailors accustomed to the long, open swell of the Atlantic or the Pacific are often dismayed with the sea conditions they encounter in the Med. What makes these conditions even more unpleasant is the fact that they often arrive during clear-weather etesian winds, when most sailors expect calm water.

As discussed above, a prudent skipper will employ specialized cruising tactics, including pre-dawn departures and motor-sailing, to outwit the meltemi or mistral while making good his northerly passage for the day. But, all too often, these tactics aren't a hundred percent effective and you find yourself offshore with fifty or sixty miles of short, nasty swell upwind of you and your destination. Typical Mediterranean sea conditions with a force five or six blow include steep, pointed wave crests that average about ten feet high after the wind has been up for several hours. If the wind force increases to a gale—as it often does with the mistral and the August meltemi—waves crest around fifteen feet and take on a definite plunging action. What exacerbates these conditions is the miserably short distance between the ranks of wave crests. On an ocean, the fetch allows the swell to spread; but there are no fetches longer than twelve hundred miles in the Mediterranean. So the seas are often short, steep, and plunging.

If you try to beat under these conditions, sailing as close to the wind as possible, several unpleasant things happen. First, you'll find that the steep advancing swells temporarily block the wind when you are down in the trough, so that your sails will momentarily luff and flog, only to be violently popped full again as the boat climbs the swell face. This causes the boat to lose way briefly, and the force of the crashing wave is more pronounced than if the boat were moving steadily with all canvas drawing. In near-gale conditions, a definite hobby-horse effect often occurs on a beat. It is not only uncomfortable and sick-making for the crew; it can also be dangerous for the rig, especially if the skipper is imprudent enough to be carrying too much sail.

Over the years, I've watched experienced charter skippers try to outwit these short Mediterranean sea conditions, and I've adapted their tactics to my own cruising. First, I plan my day's passage to include a series of tacks sailing on a near reach, not on a close-hauled rhumb line, to my destination. Generally, I sail about 65 degrees off the apparent wind, 30 degrees to leeward of *Matata*'s best close-hauled performance. I've found that we rarely hobby-horse, or lose our wind in the troughs at this point of sailing. Also, even though there's plenty of spray, we don't usually take solid water across the deck when we bear off in this manner. We may actually cover more distance across the ground by sailing a near reach, but we often arrive sooner than if we'd been beating our brains out, close-hauled against the meltemi all day.

The next tactic I've evolved is sailing with one reef in the mainsail and a small working jib for our headsail, even if the wind conditions prevailing do not dictate such reduced canvas. Sailors who've encountered the wind-against-sea conditions of the Gulf Stream, beating their way back from the Bahamas to Jupiter Inlet, will understand what I mean here. When you've got a puffy 22 or 23 knots of wind in short, steep seas, you're much better off with a reefed main and a small jib than you are trying to carry a full mainsail and genoa. With the smaller amount of sail, you do not usually bury the lee rail, and, your angle of heel decreased, you expose less topside surface to the spray and breaking waves. Over the years, timing my passages between the Gulf of Fethiye in Turkey and Rhodes—a notorious beat in the meltemi—I've learned that I actually make faster time on a near reach, undersailed with a reefed main and working jib, than I would trying to beat with a full main and genoa. Furthermore, from the managers of the large bareboat fleets in Rhodes I've learned what damage to rig and sail inventory often results when charterers attempt this beat under full sail in a meltemi.

I have also become very conscious of stowing deck equipment after fifteen years sailing the Med. All too often, boats on a summer cruise

are encumbered with wind surfers, outboards, jerry cans of water and fuel, and fishing gear, in addition to the normal deck equipment of spinnaker pole, life raft and dinghy. We still carry a fair amount of equipment on deck, but we've become almost fanatical about making sure everything is well secured. Four years ago, a vicious meltemi swell swept our deck about twenty miles east of Mykonos and ripped off our life raft canister, breaking several stout dacron lashings in the process. We spent the next two hours chasing our half-inflated raft to leeward in 40 knots of wind. After we'd finally wrestled the raft aboard, we decided we had to rethink the problem of deck equipment.

Now we carry our raft and survival kit in a soft-sided waterproof satchel on the portside quarterberth, handy to the companionway in an emergency, but protected from the violence of a decksweeping meltemi sea. We clamp our dinghy outboard on a reinforced teak mount, well aft on the portside stern pulpit, away from breaking swells. Over the years, we've also learned how best to tow our inflatable Zodiac dinghy. While some people favor keeping their dinghy well astern on a long painter, we've found that, given the cut of *Matata*'s hull, it's best to keep our Zodiac well snugged up to the transom, with the painter through a fairlead and the snout of the dinghy actually raised above the water, so that the boat rides at about a 30-degree angle. That way, if it does get flooded with a breaking wave, most of the water sloshes harmlessly out before any damage can be done. Naturally, we open the dinghy transom's bung-hole to drain the boat while it's being towed. On longer passages, we deflate and fold flat our Zodiac, lashing it securely to the coach top.

Down below, we tend to be equally fanatical about securing loose gear and stowing supplies and provisions. This discipline comes, no doubt, from running a charter boat on which our paying guests were less than seamanlike about proper stowing below and, when the meltemi puffed up, often too sick to clean up the tangled mess they'd created below by not properly stowing their personal gear, clothes, drinking glasses, etc. Now, before we sail, whether it be for an afternoon or a month cruise, we both walk through the cabins, tugging on locker doors and reaching into open bins and stowage cubbies to be sure that there are no lose wine bottles, sweaters, swimming flippers, charts, or any of the other myriad pieces of junk that always seem to come adrift when the boat starts to pound into those lumpy pyramid seas.

4. HOT-WEATHER SAILING

For five months of the year, the Mediterranean sun is *hot*. And the sun shines nearly every day. If you are sailing in this region it is almost impossible to avoid unusual exposure to the sun. In small doses, we are told, the sun is good for you. But the effects of overexposure are cumulative and much more dangerous than previously thought.

Not only is sunburn uncomfortable, but the long-range effects of this exposure include premature aging of the skin, which leaves layers of thickened, wrinkled skin after a time, the result of the body's effort to protect itself. This effect is familiar to anyone who has been around people who live and work in sunny climes . . . California, the Mediterranean. There is evidence that cumulative exposure can also lead to genetic damage. And, most importantly, skin cancer (melanoma) and other cancers triggered by skin cancer—which are the cause of death of more than 5,000 people a year in America alone—are directly related to overexposure to the ultraviolet rays of the sun.

Another danger of overexposure to the sun is damage to your vision, a disease called Pterygium. It is the result of damage to the eyes by ultraviolet light in conjunction with an abrasive irritant such as dust or salt. The resulting degradation of the eye lens—a thickening similar to cataracts—is *irreversible*.

Dehydration can be extremely serious. When there is a limited supply of liquid for consumption, as on a sailboat on a long offshore passage, there is a tendency to be overly conservative in water use. But when it is hot and dry, your body loses through perspiration much more liquid than normal, and it is essential to replace that liquid regularly.

In our many years of sailing in the Mediterranean, Malcolm and I have learned to deal with the above problems. First of all, sunburn and overexposure: we avoid long periods of exposure between nine in the morning and four in the afternoon. Easily said. The nature of sailing in the Med is to be out there, *enjoying* the sun in the middle of the day. But you can enjoy it without exposing every inch of your skin to dangerous ultraviolet rays. First, wear a brimmed hat, with a dark underside to eliminate reflected rays on your face, the most vulnerable part of your body. Wear light, long-sleeved shirts and long pants. Since this can be hot, I wear a swimsuit underneath— covering up while in the cockpit or lying on deck as the wind vane steers the boat and doffing the extra clothes to change sails or the course. The easiest and coolest arrangement I came up with (at 104 degrees in the shade) was to cut a hole in a white sheet, slip it over my head, and drape it loosely around the rest of me. That way I could tuck my feet in too, a part of my body that often gets sunburned. If I had to jump up and do something quickly, I could easily fling the cloth down the companionway and winch in a sail or grab the tiller.

As well covered as you may be, it is wise to use a sunscreen or sunblock cream. The sun protection factor should be at least "15," and the solution should contain 5% PABA. However, be aware that a recent study indicates that there may be a risk from the PABA itself; a byproduct of its chemical reaction with sunlight is the production of phototoxins. Apply the sunblock lavishly. It is available everywhere I've sailed in the Mediterranean in the last few years and can easily be replenished.

Doctors tell us that limited exposure each day will allow the skin to build up its own defense . . . the slow tanning process. But in the last forty years, people have come instead to seek "instant" tans. Now it is common for package tourists and bareboat charterers alike to feel cheated unless they are tanned almost black on their two-week vacation. Since World War II skin cancer has appeared as a new phenomena. It is predicted that by 1990 it will reach epidemic proportions. Because the effects of exposure to the ultraviolet light of the sun are cumulative, only now are people who have been overexposing themselves to the sun for years developing melanoma. Before it was fashionable to have a good tan, there was relatively little skin cancer. Our forefathers, working on farms, and their wives kept covered up and only gradually, through the seasons, were exposed to the sun's rays. Ladies, especially, were very careful to shade their faces with outsized bonnets. Long skirts, sleeves, and gloves were normal work clothes. Until the recent arrival of tourists in Greece, it was uncommon to see laborers or fishermen shirtless or in shorts. And the incidence of skin cancer has been low. With the new emphasis on showing off for the tourist girls, I've noticed that young Greek men often work shirtless or play on the beach for long hours in swim trunks. One can expect—twenty years from now—an increased incidence of skin cancer among them.

Sunglasses can help protect your eyes, but only if they actually block ultraviolet rays. (Lenses made of polycarbonate plastic do.) If you don't like to wear dark glasses, clear glasses of the same material can be obtained. Ordinary sunglasses can actually *increase* the risk of Pterygium by allowing the retina to remain wide open to the damaging rays of bright sunshine. This is a serious problem and the disease is *not* the result of cumulative exposure; it is currently being diagnosed in even young sailors. Sunglasses are a bother sometimes, but it seems to me that they're worth the bother.

As for dehydration, prevent it by drinking plenty of liquids. Don't waste the liquid from tinned food like canned fruits—drink it or use it in cooking. Any reasonable-sized boat can carry sufficient water for several days, and in the Mediterranean, unlike the middle of the Atlantic, you can easily go ashore and replenish your supply. In general, water obtained anywhere along the northern coasts of the Mediterranean is safe to drink, but there is always bottled water, cheap and pure. We carry about two cases of one-and-a-half-liter bottles of water; these can be tucked individually into many nooks and crannies about the boat. Alcohol (liquor, beer, wine) is not a replacement for liquid intake. In fact, the more alcohol you consume, the more important it is to drink an equal amount of water. This doesn't mean you can't have a beer on a hot afternoon and enjoy it. Just be sure to also have a glass of water.

Exposure to the sun and your diet interact. If you eat carrots, parsley, or limes, you will be more sensitive to the sun's effect. So, don't imbibe lime-juice cocktails unless you want a quick sunburn. Oddly, other citrus fruits do not cause this photosensitivity. In fact, they reduce the harmful effects, as do Vitamins A, E, and C and green leafy vegetables and whole grains.

Drugs you have ingested can have dangerous side-effects when combined with exposure to ultraviolet light. Most drugs have a warning on the label, or your doctor will tell you to stay out of the sun while taking a prescription drug. Be wary of tranquilizers, barbiturates, antibiotics, birth control pills, antihistamines, and Vitamin B-2 (riboflavin) in large doses.

Naturally, it is would be best to avoid the sun, wear ultraviolet protected sunglasses, eat a diet of leafy greens, throw out all the drugs, lather yourself with sunblock, keep covered from head to toe . . . but this is unrealistic. One day, even the most careful person in the world will get sunburned. A home remedy that Mal and I have used successfully on ourselves—and on many a sun-worshipping guest—is a vinegar dousing. It smells awful, but it works. As soon as possible after becoming aware of the sunburn, get out of the sun. Pour vinegar on cotton pads, liberally, and pat the sunburnt areas of your body with the vinegar. Let this dry for about fifteen minutes. Then, rinse off with fresh water. Work some after-sun exposure cream into your skin. There are many brands on the market, and they have special emollients to help the skin heal. In our experience, after the first bit of sting, your skin cools off and seldom peels.

If you are interested in how damage to the skin occurs through overexposure and the new scientific data about the dangers of overexposure to the sun, read the *Reader's Digest* July 1981 article "Sunbathing—In a New Light" by Lowell Ponte (reprints available from *Reader's Digest*).